The Ex Factor

The Ex Factor

Dealing with Your Former Spouse

Don and LaDean Houck

Fleming H. Revell
A Division of Baker Book House
Grand Rapids, Michigan 49516

©1997 by Don and LaDean Houck

Published by Fleming H. Revell
a division of Baker Book House Company
P.O. Box 6287, Grand Rapids, MI 49516-6287

Printed in the United States of America

Library of Congress Cataloging-in-Publication Data

Houck, Don
    The ex factor : dealing with your former spouse / Don and LaDean
Houck.
       p.   cm.
    Includes bibliographical references.
    ISBN 0-8007-5634-7 (pbk.)
    1. Divorced people—Psychology. 2. Divorce—Psychological aspects.
3. Divorce—Religious aspects—Christianity. 4. Separation (Psychology)
I. Houck, LaDean. II. Title.
HQ814.H73   1997
306.89—dc21   97-17572

For current information about all releases from Baker Book House, visit our web site:
http://www.bakerbooks.com

*To our former pastor, Dennis Baw,
and to our counselor, Brooke Annis*

Without your help, we would have become exes again

Contents

Acknowledgments   9
Introduction   11

1   Wrong or Wronged   15
2   A Light or a Judge   23
3   Holding On or Letting Go   31
4   Barriers or Bridges   41
5   Terrible or Tolerant   51
6   Conflict or Creativity   65
7   Bitter or Better   77
8   Warfare or "Well-fare"   89
9   Control or Compassion   101
10   Petty or Partners   109

A Closing Blessing   123
Recommended Resources   125
Notes   126
Blended Blessings   127

Acknowledgments

We wish to thank the following people without whose help, love, and concern this book would have never been.

- Dr. David George, our pastor, who keeps us accountable to the integrity of spiritual and biblical truth. He continually adds creativity to what we write and demands that we confront sensitive issues in a straightforward manner.
- Dr. Ed Laymance, our counselor and friend, who saw what we wrote through the eyes of a counselor and encouraged us to stay focused on our principles. He is a man of few words, but when he speaks—we listen.
- Kay Marshall, our wordsmith and friend, who constantly encouraged us, critiqued our work, and understood the message of our hearts. She helped us fine-tune our original manuscript.
- Our advisory council, who constantly prays for us and advises us.
- Pam Campbell, our editor, who spent hours on the phone with us as we worked through structure, grammar, humor, and kindness. We feel as if we have a soul-

mate. We looked forward to our weekly phone conversations.

- Bill Petersen, our publisher, who believed in us, was patient with us, understood our hearts, and allowed us the time needed to write a book like this. We are forever grateful for his desire to minister to others.

- Ken and Betty Kielbas, our friends, who allowed us spur-of-the-moment access to their input, which we needed during the editing process.

- All of those who were willing to share their stories, some of which are still painful.

- George, my ex, and Paulette, my wife-in-law, who have been very gracious in allowing us to share experiences that included them.

- Our family, who let us write about them: our children—David, Paul, and Trey; our daughters-in-law—Keely and Sarah; our grandchildren—Kalese, Michael, and Kalen.

Introduction

earning to deal with an ex-mate effectively is a problem all divorced people must face. Exes factor in every facet of our lives, whether we want them to or not, and especially when children are involved.

Sometimes the situations we have to deal with regarding our exes seem impossible to live with or to resolve. Despair often drives us to throw ourselves completely on God's mercy, and that is exactly what God wants us to do. His mercy does make a difference by helping the healing process to begin. As we continue the healing process, God's mercy is always there watering our growth.

We will be using our personal experiences with our exes as well as examples from others to illustrate principles. We do not pass judgment or seek justification—we are using these experiences merely to illumine our points. It has taken years for us to be able to recall some of them without bitterness.

Child-napping, abusive behavior, and death threats are cases of extreme behavior exhibited by some exes. In these kinds of cases, the only relationship that can occur is through the legal system. We seek to address solutions for less extreme cases. We are aware that not everyone with an ex is remarried or is ready to consider that step. We are also sensitive to those of you who are single again and wish to remain that way.

During our marriage to each other, we have experienced both harmony and discord with our exes. It hasn't been sugar and spice all the time, but with a lot of determination, the relationships have become workable. We haven't always achieved the results we wanted, but we have learned to live with limited expectations and the satisfaction of acceptable arrangements.

Your decision to read this book is a step in making "ex-hood" work. All family situations are unique in their makeup and especially so when exes are involved. We urge you to use your creativity to make the principles you find here work for your situation.

For those of you who are neck-deep in ex-hood, you will understand why names have been changed to protect the guilty.

Before You Begin

You can have a harmonious relationship with your ex-mate by working through the principles outlined in this book, provided your ex-mate is agreeable. As you receive teaching from the Lord in these pages and allow it to take root in your life, you will change. What you accomplish will be most difficult, but you also will have the blessing and companionship of God on your journey. This means you will have the freedom to not make every situation with your ex a power struggle. This will enable you to accomplish more, with positive results.

Our prayer for you is that you will come to know God in a new freshness and freedom. We also are praying that you will be able to look at your ex-mate with new compassion, forgiveness, and caring. May you have the same peace we and others have found from the daily hassle with exes.

"Being confident of this, that he who began a good work in you will carry it on to completion until the day of Christ Jesus" (Philippians 1:6).

Wrong or Wronged

averne began removing pictures and other items from the walls. She had contracted for some minor remodeling on her house.

She was in a state of despair. Her marriage of twenty-three years had ended, and she felt that she had lost most of her life. Though her college-age children, a son and a daughter, had chosen to stay with her in the house she was given in the divorce decree, she was still in a world of hurt.

As she sorted through the remains of her life, Laverne recalled all the years of affairs by her husband, Tom, and the toll those liaisons had taken on their marriage. Tom always seemed to be looking for something else, something more exciting. Life to him was an endless quest for one more new thrill. Laverne knew he was bored with their marriage and that he felt cheated because life was not all he wanted it to be, but she felt helpless to do anything about the situation. Tom finally filed for divorce. Laverne had not wanted it because, as bad as the marriage was, she really *did* love Tom.

Throughout her unhappy marriage Laverne had consoled herself with her faith and her service to God. Though Tom had attended church with her, she had come to view herself as spiritual leader of the family. She dutifully read her

Bible, regularly taught Sunday school, and sang in the choir. She was willing to help whenever needed and was gifted in helping others through their struggles. Her friends at church just couldn't understand how Tom could leave such a faithful Christian wife and so quickly remarry someone else.

In her sorting, Laverne focused on the plaques, each with a family member's name and its spiritual meaning. As she removed her "Laverne" plaque, she noticed something on the back. She read these words:

> Laverne means hypocrite. For twenty-three years, you never brought your Christianity into our home. I suffered for years from your neglect!
>
> Tom

Laverne went livid with anger and resentment. *How could he say such a thing! How small of him to not be aware of how much I have done for this marriage!* Other terms describing him flew through her thoughts. She found herself shaking, unable to speak.

Later, as she began to calm down, a small voice inside her spoke. *If you are the wronged one and not the one in the wrong, why are you so intensely defensive? What is there for you to be concerned about?*

Lord, is it I? asked Laverne. *Have I also been in the wrong here?*

She knew the answer was yes even as she asked. She had been able to cope so far by viewing herself as the wronged one and Tom as the one in the wrong. This sudden revelation showed a whole new facet of her life. She dissolved into a puddle, going from condemnation to crying to depression for several days. It took her many weeks to be able to face the task before her: changing her mental, emotional view of God as well as her spiritual relationship to God.

Laverne began to ask herself what she had done wrong in her marriage. The answer was simple, but not easy. First, she realized she had never developed intimate, spiritual communication with Tom. They talked very little about spiritual things except when she was "teaching" the family spiritual truths. As she reviewed the years of their marriage, she realized that mostly she had done this to make herself feel worthy and "spiritual"!

Next, she recognized that she had tried to live a perfect life before Tom, so that everything projected the proper image of a happy marriage and a Christian family. She had never shared her fears, weaknesses, and disappointments with her husband, who knew them well. By denying her human failings and trying to be "strong," she weakened her position with her husband. He eventually sought out someone he felt was more honest.

Her new knowledge didn't make Laverne feel worthless, but it took her a long time to forgive herself, to ask for God's forgiveness, and to move on with her life.

Laverne still serves in the church, but her devotion is to God, not to service. She also has become a more open, honest person. Her children now perceive her as more human, a real person who communicates truth. Her relationship with her ex is based on honesty and an understanding that what seems right and wrong to us is often conditional on our viewpoint in a particular situation. Sometimes, both people may be right.

All Wrong or All Right

No one is ever all wrong or all right. We all have strengths and shortcomings. No matter how we try to convince ourselves otherwise, we all know that divorce is the result of *two* people not being able to deal effectively with the nitty-gritty issues in marriage. It is human nature for us to feel more accepted by society, and especially the church, if we are perceived as the wronged party rather than as in the wrong. The person who removes himself or herself from the relationship is sometimes viewed by the church as the offender, branded with a big *D* on the forehead.

Those of us who have been divorced know that each party is wrong at some point in the deterioration of the marriage relationship. We have lived with divorce and know the havoc it creates in the lives of all involved. We know firsthand why God hates divorce. We do not justify divorce theologically or any other way. But we must deal with ex-mates from the viewpoint of what we can do now to make things better.

Perhaps the most powerful wrong we both committed in our previous marriages was to not nurture them. We thought we were nurturing because we did all the special occasion and anniversary things. Neither of us wanted to admit that what we had done—or not done—in our first marriages was damaging. We both finally had to come to terms with the fact that we had been wrong—not just in order to release the past, but to strengthen our present marriage.

No one is ever all wrong or all right.

Until we were willing to take responsibility for our parts in the disasters, the amicable relationships we were trying to build with our exes were unsuccessful.

Regardless of the part played in the divorce, both parties feel they have been wronged. We must get past these feelings of "poor me" in order to be able to deal with our ex-mates. While we could get great satisfaction in hearing our exes say, "I was wrong," it is probably not going to happen. We cannot depend on what the ex does or doesn't do. We have to take charge of our lives so that we get healthy within ourselves and "right" with God.

Begin claiming this Scripture: "Let us strip off anything that slows us down or holds us back, and especially those sins that wrap themselves so tightly around our feet and trip us up; and let us run with patience the particular race that God has set before us" (Hebrews 12:1 TLB).

Our friend Del Brewer puts it this way: "How much rejection and devastation we experience depends on whether we are the 'leave-ee' or the 'left-ee.' I think the one who leaves the marriage has an easier time initiating contact with the ex-mate. The one left behind seems to experience the most devastation and rejection and has a harder time initiating or responding to contact with the ex-mate. My faith in God has given me the peace to turn loose of any effect my former marriage might have on my present life."

DON: What Del has said is very true in our "ex-lives." I was the left-ee and refused to make any contact for many years. I think my ex-wife thought that filing for divorce would shake me out of my tree.

LADEAN: I was the leave-ee and made the first contact with my ex regarding our son's welfare.

The next big step is to accept that our ex-mates are sometimes right. When we feel we always have to be right, we are in bondage to our intellect. Only in our spirits can we gain the freedom to allow our exes to be right sometimes— and that freedom comes from the Lord. Recognizing that our exes are right does not mean we give up our beliefs or convictions. It more often means our exes can be right also!

Lectures and Lies

Admitting that we were in the wrong may feel so potentially damaging to our sense of our worth that we have to create unreal pictures of our past and present lives to justify our actions. These unreal pictures are lies. As we listen to what God is teaching us through life, we can learn to release the pain we have carried with us from the past and begin to deal with life honestly. We must journey from lecturing, embellishing, and lying to listening, learning, and growing.

DON: At the time LaDean and I married, I was just beginning to know the real me. I had just entered my forties and was finally confronting some habits begun in my teen years and carried throughout my adulthood. I so much wanted to be significant to other people that I sometimes embellished parts of my past to look heroic. I even manufactured some things to add to my image. I viewed all situations only as they filtered through my pretend past.

Since I was so preoccupied with my past and not maturing as a person, I had many unreal expectations and attitudes regarding marriage and parenting. For example, I had to be right about everything, and I needed to feel the power of being in control. Being in control meant that I had to straighten out everyone else, especially my wife and children. In order to do that, there was a lecture for every situation. When facts wouldn't support my lecture, I could manufacture a new set of facts so I could always be right as I helped everyone else to be perfect.

These expectations and attitudes were a big problem as I dealt with my ex-wife and my two sons. They had lived with me and knew more of the real me than I realized. I now believe my falseness was a big factor in my ex's decision to live her life apart from me. And I never fooled my sons—they knew. Had I not been that way, I perhaps would not be an ex now.

After my divorce, I used this mechanism to make the whole divorce process my ex's fault. I dragged a very convincing pity party around with me for years, so at any time I could wallow in it and always appear justified in my misery. My emotional baggage contained all my pretend past heroics, so whenever I got into any kind of relationship struggle or crisis, I could remind the world what a great guy I had been.

Only since I have been willing to listen to the voice of God and to what life has been trying to teach me about myself have I been able to conquer this character flaw. This process began with an overwhelming desire on my part to be emotionally and spiritually healthy. I soon realized that was what God planned all along. He wanted me to allow him to build his perfect healthy life in me.

God began using several people, his Holy Word, and some self-help books to open my inner man to the need to mature. God has used LaDean in many significant and sometimes very uncomfortable ways to reveal these difficult areas of my life. Often these confrontations happened during one of our screaming discussions. When emotions are out of control, it is difficult to hear God's voice seeking to teach us a godly principle for our lives. However, God has been relentless in his pursuit of change in me. As I have been willing to change, it has been easier for me to recognize God's voice. I am eternally grateful for LaDean's willingness to stay with me long enough for me to begin growing up. As I get healthy and mature, she is free to be all that God intended her to be. She truly has become my best friend. The Scripture that became precious to me during this growth passage is from Galatians: "I have been crucified with Christ and I no longer live, but Christ lives in me. The life I live in the body, I live by faith in the Son of God, who loved me and gave himself for me" (2:20).

Another part of the ongoing growth process is the daily inner battle to refrain from slipping back into my old thought patterns. My freedom has been bought by Jesus, so slavery to the old ways is my choice. Another Scripture that sustains me is: "It is for freedom that Christ has set us free. Stand firm, then, and do not let yourselves be burdened again by a yoke of slavery" (Galatians 5:1).

Since my ex-wife has been around me very little since the divorce, she has not observed the depth of change in me. But, based on her thank-you note regarding my attitude and actions when she lost her mother, I know she saw a different me. Both of my sons have conveyed to me in different conversations that they realize I am not the same old dad they used to know.

Listen and Learn

As we walk by faith, we act on what God is showing us. God is constantly seeking to show us how to treat our exes as Christ would. If we don't allow God to control our thinking, we are unable to hear him speak to us. As we listen to God, we will be able to treat our exes with compassion and caring firmness. This results in change for us! If we are listening and learning, then we are not lecturing anyone or listening to the lies society tells us about how to treat our exes.

A Light or a Judge

LADEAN: I lit the candle and took my place as mother of the groom. The wedding was beginning. As I sat there remembering Trey's life and all that had happened to us, I was aware of sobbing next to me on the pew. I passed tissues to my ex-husband, George, and to Trey's stepmother, Paulette. I was so lost in my thoughts that I forgot to pass the tissues to my husband, Don.

Watching the candle flicker, I wondered how much George and I had been lights in Trey's life. When George and I divorced, we were intensely critical of each other. It took six years and lots of changes for us to begin talking to each other without throwing jabs. Now, seventeen years since our divorce, I felt so thankful that we could sit together in the same pew and share the wedding experience of our only son. *How sad it must be,* I thought, *for those who must deal with the additional pressures of competition and annoyance with an ex at an already stressful situation like a wedding.*

The rehearsal dinner last night was so much fun. Just exactly what all of us needed. Trey's four parents had worked together planning, decorating, and cleaning up for the event. At the end of the evening as George and I settled up with the caterer, George said,

"You've done a good job." I think he meant with raising Trey as well as with the rehearsal dinner. He had been gracious enough to allow me to take the lead with the preparations but was there to assist, suggest, and pay his part. I did a much better job now of including him, asking his opinion, and taking his suggestions than when Trey was in elementary school. I felt the waves of shame wash over me as I recalled how I had refused to allow George to see Trey's report cards.

How times had changed! Paulette and I had shared rides to the wedding showers and had been together through all the festivities. We were amused at those who had difficulty deciding which one of us was Trey's mother. Some determined that Paulette was my sister or friend. We laughed as I introduced her as Trey's other mom or stepmom and as my wife-in-law.

While the four of us don't socialize on an ongoing basis, we had been able to be together and enjoy the occasion of this wedding. I believe God softened my heart *and* George's.

The trumpets started to play as Trey's bride, Sarah, walked down the aisle. When Trey's voice quivered as he began his vows, I prayed for him. Trey and Sarah stood at the unity candle taking the one I had lit and the one her mother had lit and lighting their own. They blew out our candles so the unity candle was the only one remaining. Had George and I been lights? I think so.

God's Light

"God is light; in him there is no darkness at all. If we claim to have fellowship with him yet walk in the darkness, we lie and do not live by the truth. But if we walk in the light, as he is in the light, we have fellowship with one another, and the blood of Jesus, his Son, purifies us from all sin" (1 John 1:5–7).

As George and I were drawn to God's light, our manner of approaching and working with each other began to change. We noticed we were becoming less quick to condemn. We made the decision to listen and learn. This was moving from darkness to light.

It is important to remember some things we all know. Darkness obscures our pathway, paralyzes our walk, and creates fear, which is the foundation of anger. When we choose to be light, we bring illumination to our pathway, action to our walk, and confidence in our direction. These verses give us the path to follow when we make this decision to live in the light: "Thy word is a lamp to my feet and a light to my path" (Psalm 119:105); "I saw that wisdom is better than folly, just as light is better than darkness" (Ecclesiastes 2:13).

As George and I were drawn to God's light, our manner of approaching and working with each other began to change.

By being lights we establish a pattern in the relationship that our exes can follow, if they choose. If we listen rather than challenge, it will make it easier for them to listen to us. When we are in the light, we become examples. In dealing with our exes, we will do this in many different ways, but whenever we make the choice, it is to a higher, better, more peaceful way of life.

In his book *Principle-Centered Leadership,* Stephen Covey says: "The challenge is to be a light, not a judge . . . a model, not a critic."[1] When working with our exes, it is most helpful to be a light rather than a judge or a critic. Modeling good behavior puts a whole new perspective on ex-hood.

Being a Judge

When we assume the role of judge, our focus is on our self-preservation and we make others responsible for our problems. Society accepts a judgmental attitude in our relationship to our exes, but God doesn't as evidenced in Matthew 7:1–5, "Do not judge lest you be judged. For in the way you judge, you will be judged; and by your standard of measure, it will be measured to you. And, why do you look at the speck that is in your brother's eye, but do not notice the log that is in your own eye? Or how can you say to your brother, 'Let me take the speck out of your eye,' and behold, the log is in your own eye? You hypocrite, first take the log out of your own eye and then you will see clearly to take the speck out of your brother's eye" (NASB). A judgmental attitude results in more resistance and few solutions to problems.

The person who judges:

1. examines another's hopes, fears, failures, and weaknesses, to be used against them in the future;
2. determines another's thoughts, emotions, motives, and feelings, so that the one who judges can control any situation;
3. sentences others through condemnation, never being right, and being against what the judge wants, in order to justify the position of the one who judges.

A woman confessed to us at one of our conferences that both she and her ex-husband told their daughter they would not come to her wedding if the other was there. They both thought this would force the daughter to make a decision to choose them. The daughter and her fiancé ran off to Oklahoma to get married by a justice of the peace. There was no wedding for anyone to go to. With many tears the mother lamented her unwillingness to control her bitterness toward her ex long enough to enjoy her only daughter's wedding.

Divorced people often judge themselves harshly and can be their own worst critics. This self-condemnation leads to guilt, which may require professional help to overcome. Only God's forgiveness and cleansing can bring us spiritual freedom from our past. We must exercise faith and believe that God can change us and remove the need to judge.

We should not confuse judging others with spiritual discernment. Judging others condemns while spiritual discernment reveals truth. God gives us discernment to enable us to make wise choices.

What Do Our Exes Owe Us?

We can easily feel that our ex-mates owe us something for the pain we have experienced. As long as we filter our thoughts regarding our exes through pain and anger, we will be looking to collect our debts. Whatever we think they owe us can get in the way of our ability to listen and learn. In reality, our exes owe us the same thing we owe them— nothing, other than common courtesy. The Golden Rule of doing unto others as we would have them do unto us is as good as it gets for many ex-relationships.

Many of us developed a sense of entitlement as children when we were given cookies, toys, or TV to keep us occupied. As adults, this feeling can lead to unreal expectations about marriage, parenting, and relationships. We often operate within our relationships out of a desire for our own comfort and satisfaction rather than a scriptural foundation of giving to others to bring glory to God. Ex-hood magnifies our feelings of entitlement and makes it difficult for us to be givers. We feel we have already given enough. Jesus gave us this example, "Not so with you. Instead, whoever wants to become great among you must be your servant, and whoever wants to be first must be your slave—just as the Son of Man did not come to be served, but to serve, and to give his life as a ransom for many" (Matthew 20:26–28).

This is not to say we are to be slaves to our ex-mates. We must recognize that our relationship with our exes has limitations. Our servanthood is to our heavenly Father and his will. That does not mean we allow ourselves to be used or abused, but we can extend kindness to our exes. For many of us, just being kind to our exes is a real exercise in faith. Exercising faith builds our inner strength.

Faith in God

Faith is believing without proof. Faith is hearing God's Word and acting as though it were before us. Faith sometimes gives us glimpses of hope to affirm we are following in God's pathway. We must listen to the voice of God in little things. Faith is an attitude always accompanied by action. Faith must be exercised in all things, not just in crises. Living by faith separates those who know about God from those who know God personally. How? People who know about God can only focus on what God does—experience. Those who know God personally and intimately focus on who God is in their lives and where he is guiding them—relationship.

Colleen had been struggling for several years to improve her attitude toward her ex-husband. They had never been able to talk about the children without ending up in a fight. Colleen began to realize she could not change her ex, so she had to change herself. She sought a more personal relationship with God. Having been a Christian since childhood, she was only now beginning to know God personally. As she grew spiritually, she began to realize even though she could not change her ex, she could pray for peace between them. Colleen determined to not give up. She listened to God and treated her ex with compassion and firmness.

The first evidence of her faith at work came through her former mother-in-law.

"You know, Bill," she told her son, "Colleen could have withheld the children from visiting us, but she never has. I appreciate her kindness in spite of the contentious attitude I see in you. I believe it would help the whole situation if you would work harder at getting along with her regarding the children."

Bill was bothered by his mother's words and, after some introspection, he realized his mother had a point. About the same time, Bill and Colleen's children confronted him about how he talked about their mother. They never heard their mom say the kinds of nasty things he said about her, and they wished he would not talk about her that way any more.

Colleen began to see a different attitude from her ex. Everything was still not perfect, and they disagreed over some issues, but there was less bitterness in their conversations concerning the children. Colleen realized building her faith in God not only had changed her attitude, but had brought about a dramatic change in her family as well. She had become a light.

Holding On
or Letting Go

The summer sun warmed Christy's back as she basked on the beach next to her husband, Ken. For the first time since their marriage five years ago, Ken and Christy vacationed by themselves, relaxing and enjoying nine days of romance—long walks on the beach and hours cuddling while they shared their dreams and plans for the future. Christy had never felt more fulfilled and at peace. Life was good and all was well with the world. Tomorrow they would return to the routines at home, and already Christy felt sad about ending this second honeymoon.

"Mommy, Mommy." Jason's voice jerked Christy back to the present. "Why are you crying, Mommy?" Jason's face puckered with concern as he patted Christy's arm. "Are you hurt?"

"No, sweetheart, I'm not hurt. I was just remembering something that makes me sad." Christy brushed a tear from her cheek, then forced a smile and kissed her son's forehead.

Christy had been divorced five months and found it difficult to deal with her memories. The hardest memories to deal with were the pleasant ones, like the vacation at the beach, and Christy struggled with how she should feel about those good times in her past. She had tried to forget them, but it just didn't work. They still haunted her.

Christy realized it was going to take a long time to sort out all of these feelings and memories. As she watched Jason build his sand castle, she thought, *Sooner or later he's going to want to know why Daddy stopped living with us. How am I going to explain the truth to him? I don't want him to think he is responsible in any way. How do I keep him from being scarred for life?*

Anger welled inside as Christy recalled the painful experiences of the last year.

On this day, Christy would never have believed that this anger would eventually help her deal with her pain.

Hide-and-Seek

Christy had experienced something common to all divorced people—a surge of confusing emotions, brought on by a poignant memory (good or bad) of married life. Like Christy, we try to convince ourselves that the bad memories outweigh the good ones. It becomes a game of hide-and-seek—mask the good memories and focus on the bad ones.

We do not need to live in the past, but the past is part of us, and we only fool ourselves when we deny it. We trick ourselves into believing that we cannot deal with our ex in a spirit of harmony.

In addition, society accepts and even encourages feelings of distrust, anger, disgust, and dislike toward a former spouse. TV and movies, as well as books and magazine articles, all promote ex bashing. We can buy this package of bitterness, hoping that by doing so we will erase all memories of an ex from our lives. Or we can seek, with God's help, the silver lining of a relationship gone bad. Anger and bitterness cannot erase some facts from our lives. Let's face it, at one time we loved these people enough to pledge our lives till death do us part. What happened to that love? When a divorce happens, does that mean there are no good memories? Should we try to erase that wonderful vacation we took to the mountains or the beach? What about the times when we were so close and made so many plans for our future? If that union created children, were those not joyous occasions?

Defining and separating what we need to hold on to and what we need to let go of are very complicated but are necessary for healing.

Holding On

Allowing memories to hold us and holding on to memories are two different things. Memories hold us when we live in them to the extent that they negatively dominate our thinking. We convince ourselves that being angry about the bad helps us let go of the relationship. In addition, we tend to hold on to the negative because those are the most recent memories. Besides, reliving the good memories often hurts.

Most people do not think they can hold on to their memories and still let go of the person. Keeping a memory close does not mean we are still wrapped up in the relationship. Holding on to some good memories is important, however, because this validates a portion of our lives that cannot be denied. When hate is what we let go of, it changes how we perceive our ex-partners. Some of the couples in our conferences actually perceive their exes as distant relatives. Keep in mind, it really is all right to show compassion, concern, and caring for this used-to-be.

Memories are built on incidents and situations that are permanent. Their effect on us now is less significant, but

Defining and separating what we need to hold on to and what we need to let go of are very complicated but are necessary for healing.

they can affect our current relationships. Many mates feel very threatened if the new spouse has fond memories of past family happenings. We must grow enough emotionally not to be threatened in the present relationship by a mate's memories of the past. We cannot erase them from our mates' minds. The present relationship can be damaged by our unwillingness to accept the obvious— that we each had a former marriage and a family different from the present one. Discussing the happy memories of our former marriages requires us to be tolerant and loving toward each other, realizing this discussion in no way demeans or limits

the relationship with the new spouse. The fear of remembrance is removed.

Letting Go

The important process of letting go deals with guilt, anger, and the hold our former relationship has on us. Guilt may result from feelings of failure for our part in the divorce or from the pain of feeling inadequate in our relationship skills regarding our ex-spouse. Some people experience guilt because they think they are supposed to want to get back together, but the desire is not there. These feelings can develop into anger at ourselves, at the situation, at God, and at other people. Feelings of failure combined with the pain of our inability to make the relationship work often lead to anger that permeates our lives. The result is the black cloud of guilt. Guilt gets in the way of the process of letting go. Letting go is simply readjusting the perceptions we have of the past relationship with the ex-mate and of how that relationship affects our present lives.

Letting go is a threefold process: redefine, reconcile, and release.

Redefine the Relationship

We must redefine our relationships with our ex-mates in three areas: (1) our perception of the relationship, (2) the depth of the relationship, and (3) the future of the relationship.

Because of divorce, our perception of a one-flesh relationship has been legally terminated, but the emotional termination takes longer. Each individual has to come to the point of emotional termination on his or her own. However, emotional termination from your ex does not mean emotional separation from your children.

Don had a hard time separating emotionally from his ex-wife. He was not dealing with romantic feelings but with an emotional involvement spanning twenty-one years. The children were a big part of that relationship, and he was afraid his kids would have nothing to do with him.

Many absent parents are fearful that they will be ostracized by their children, so they allow the emotional ties with the ex-mates to exist in order to feel close to their children. They tend to make excuses for the negative actions of their exes in order to not lose with the children. The difficulty comes when we are unable to separate our former romantic feelings for our ex-mates from the task-oriented business of raising our children.

The depth of the feeling for that other person has nothing to do with the children. It has to do with the relationship. This is why even when there are no children, there are still strong feelings that seem to haunt exes. Sometimes these feelings take years to get over. What could have been, what was but isn't, maybes and ifs all cloud our memories for a long time.

Janie sat in our den telling us about her ex-husband. There were no children from their marriage, but she is still tormented by memories of their relationship.

"I just can never seem to get away from him in my mind," she confessed. "Every time I try to get close to someone new, thoughts of him interfere."

These memories can affect every new relationship we enter. Our ability to get close, to trust, to dream, to plan for the future are all affected by our memories of our ex-mates, whether we consciously recognize it or not. Our memories will not cease to exist, but our choice is how much and in what way those memories control and affect our lives.

We must set a goal for the future—that our present relationships and actions will not be controlled by our memories, whether children are involved or not. Achieving this goal frees us to get on with our lives.

Steps for Achieving the Goal

- Remember   the memory for what it is—in the past, permanent, and part of me.
- Recognize   what it can do to me now—positive or negative.
- Reject   the destruction that can happen.
- Reassemble the part the memory plays in my life today.

Redefining the perception, the depth, and the future of a relationship is a priority in the holding on, letting go process. Some exes can maintain a close, compassionate relationship, but for others this is too painful. Each individual must determine the depth and future of any relationship with an ex-mate.

Reconcile Feelings toward Your Ex

"Did you see the parents talking together, just like normal people, and even smiling?" Don's son David asked his brother, Paul, at a family gathering.

"Yes," Paul replied, "I observed this phenomenon, a real first."

DON: This conversation was my first awareness of bitterness, and it was hard to swallow. I knew the bitterness was mine, but I did not want to admit that I had carried this for eight years. I had refused to allow any kind of harmony to develop with my ex-wife because my feelings were still captive to the hurt I carried. I had not fooled anyone. Even my grown children were well aware of my feelings.

In order to find peace, our need to reconcile our feelings toward an ex-mate must be greater than the anger and pain. This need may be rooted in the desire for a relationship with children or extended family, or even for mental health. I realized I wanted to be healthy, and the old bitterness was stunting my growth.

LADEAN: I, on the other hand, worked through this process more quickly because I wanted my son to become a healthy young man. I realized I must "get over it" if Trey was to be healthy. This may sound cold, but sometimes people have to rise above a situation. I refused to allow past pain to prevent me from working with my ex. However, that same pain kept me emotionally sharp when negotiating with him. I changed my focus from being bitter to enhancing Trey's mental and emotional health. The more I focused on Trey being OK, the less I felt the need to seek revenge. By redefining the situation, my attitude improved also.

What happens if the relationship is so severed that a social reconciliation cannot take place? Then we must make that reconciliation take place in our intellect and emotions. This situation is more likely when there are no children involved and the exes have no potential contact with each other. When we are not with our exes on a daily basis, we can forget the devastation of the physical and emotional destruction in which we were living. Emotional desperation consumes us if we do not make a conscious effort to get on with life. When abandonment takes place, feelings of guilt creep into our consciousness—if this or that had happened, we could have made it. Our memories can now serve as a positive force to remind us that we are on a new path in life, and God's path is always one to health and freedom.

Release the Desire for Revenge

One woman we interviewed described how she felt a great satisfaction of revenge when she mailed boxes of her ex-husband's pornographic literature to his mother, whom she felt had helped destroy their relationship. She believed her mother-in-law had always viewed her son as a saint and the daughter-in-law as incompetent and below him. Ex-wives are more inclined to feel vengeance and anger than closure and resolution. Because of lowered social status and economic instability, many divorced women carry an "attitude" for years.

We must release the desire for revenge—that our exes must somehow pay for our anguish. One ex-wife got so mad at her husband that she stormed out to her car, put it in gear, and rammed his pickup—not once, but three times! He stood in the doorway of his house with his mouth open, not believing what he was seeing. Revenge takes a lot of energy that would have been better directed into positive action.

The Bible has much to say regarding releasing revenge. In Matthew 5:23–26, Jesus tells us to obey the law of reconciliation so that we are not controlled by anger and so that our relationship with God is unaffected. We also are instructed to make friends quickly with our opponent so we are not thrown in prison, therefore being controlled by the bitterness we will not release.

Steps for Releasing Revenge

Since the desire for vengeance is internal, much of what we do to release it is within us. We can work through some steps to overcome the desire for revenge.

- Realize   revenge is destructive to my own purposes.
- Focus   on what is positive in my life—children, friends, my mental, spiritual, and emotional health.
- Decide   not to seek revenge.
- Change   my thought patterns from destruction to rebuilding whatever business must be done with my ex. This could include children, a business, property, etc.
- Reinforce the feelings of freedom I'll find as I release the desire for revenge.

LADEAN: When my ex-husband married and later divorced his second wife, I realized that the number two wife had been everything I ever wished for him . . . and more! This was a great release for me to know that it was not my job to persecute my ex. I realized I had directed my hatred at my ex when in reality I hated the fact that we were divorced, hated the situation surrounding the divorce, and hated the havoc it caused for the people we cared about. I confused hating the situation with hating the person. I found closure in my ongoing struggle with revenge as I recalled and claimed this promise of God: "Do not take revenge, my friends, but leave room for God's wrath, for it is written: 'It is mine to avenge; I will repay,' says the Lord" (Romans 12:19).

Deuteronomy 32:35 (quoted by Paul in Romans 12) reminds us that vengeance is God's and not ours. We are not to execute retribution for being hurt but must leave that to God.

The power of these Scriptures is evident. We must realize that if we continue to harbor revenge and hatred in our hearts, we build a barrier between us and God's will for our lives. Building bridges with other people is an important factor in our spiritual health. When we objectively look at the effects of vengeance on our lives and the lives of our families, we will see that revenge is just not worth the consequences.

40

Barriers or Bridges

Martha was busy cooking dinner while her thoughts were on her son Randy's wedding, which was only a week away. It had been a real battle trying to incorporate all that her ex-husband, Mark, and his new wife, Joan, wanted to do regarding the wedding. Now with only a week to go, she could see that the whole event might actually take place fairly smoothly. She quietly prayed that her son and soon-to-be daughter-in-law would allow God to be the center of their lives and that they would never experience the devastation of divorce.

The ringing phone brought her back to the tasks at hand. She cradled the phone on her shoulder while she stirred the stew. It was Mark calling about last minute details. They seemed to be communicating well until . . .

"Oh, by the way, at the rehearsal dinner Friday night, I'm going to include a birthday celebration for Joan. I know that means some extra people and more of her family, but I'm sure you can understand, can't you?"

Martha felt her overload valve giving way, but she reminded herself that this was her son's wedding, so to keep peace at this late date, she agreed. After hanging up, she burst into tears of disappointment and anger.

"Now I know why I'm not married to him anymore!" she sobbed.

She couldn't keep from voicing her feelings, even if it was just to the telephone. Mark's announcement felt like a slap in the face.

When her husband, Rod, got home, she told him the news, and they prayed and promised together not to allow this incident to spoil the wedding for Randy or for them.

Martha and Rod enjoyed the rehearsal and the wedding in spite of the stress of that final week. In fact, Joan even called to thank Martha for making the occasion so joyful. Martha and Rod realized that they had grown both personally and spiritually through the whole situation. By refusing to give in to their feelings, they learned they could endure more than they thought possible. They built a bridge within themselves, based on their love for Randy that overshadowed their own pettiness. They chose to allow the outside pressures to bring them together and to view the situation through a changed attitude.

The Growth Factor

Our attitude determines whether the past and present experiences in our lives and the lives of our mates become barriers or bridges to our personal growth. When we filter everything regarding our ex through our past emotions of pain and anger, we will always be in conflict. When we can't change a situation, we still have a choice to change our attitude about the situation.

Anytime we feel a wrong has been done against us, only the Spirit of Christ can keep us from regressing into a pity party resulting in bitterness. Our desire for freedom from the pain caused by our anger must become more important than revenge.

One of the toughest questions we will ever ask ourselves is: "How would Christ treat my ex-mate?" In his letter to the Christians at Philippi, Paul warned: "Each of you should look not only to your own interests, but also to the interests of others. Your attitude should be the same as that of Christ Jesus" (Philippians 2:4–5).

This Scripture does not say, "unless you are divorced." God is not interested in our efforts to justify our positions. He is aware that both of us have sinned. However, there is hope.

Growth in Regard to Forgiveness

Forgiveness is the beginning of growth. We begin by asking God's forgiveness for our part in bringing us to the point of divorce. A great promise Scripture to remember is 1 John 1:9: "If we confess our sins, he is faithful and just and will forgive us our sins and purify us from all unrighteousness." A critical part of forgiveness is to confess. Trying to justify is not even close to confession. When we confess, we agree with God about our sins, with no alibis. God forgives us on the basis of Christ's sacrifice on the cross.

> *Forgiveness is the beginning of growth.*

Sometimes forgiving ourselves is more difficult than accepting God's forgiveness. Often, we get bogged down in guilt and pain to the point that we become unable to grow and progress in life. It may help to claim and accept fully the last part of 1 John 1:9—it is God who cleanses us "from all unrighteousness." If God has cleansed and purified us, who are we to reject the freedom and joy for which he paid with his life?

Forgiving ourselves often happens in layers, like peeling an onion. We take the layers off one at a time to reveal new vulnerability in our lives. Peeling the layers often brings tears because it is painful, but the tears sometimes fertilize necessary growth.

LADEAN: I began the forgiveness of myself and my ex-husband when we met together regarding issues concerning our son, Trey. We met at a local restaurant with a written agenda, and the only topic discussed was how to help Trey be a healthy young man. As these meetings progressed, I was able to forgive myself and my ex-husband. I became aware of how much both of us had changed. I eventually was able to fully forgive myself and my ex with the following confession: "We are both very different people now, and I like the me I am now much better than the me I was then. Those experiences helped shape the person I am now."

This confession was not at all a cop-out for divorce but was my perspective as one who had grown through the darkest days of her life and could now realize the promise of Job 11:13–17.

> If you devote your heart to him
> and stretch out your hands to him,
> If you put away the sin that is in your hand
> and allow no evil to dwell in your tent,
> then you will lift up your face without shame;
> you will stand firm and without fear.
> You will surely forget your trouble,
> recalling it only as waters gone by.
> Life will be brighter than noonday,
> and darkness will become like morning.

An unforgiving spirit in me crumbles the bridge of forgiveness over which I must pass. I did not realize until after the fact that God used my willingness to forgive my ex-husband to build a bridge in my spirit.

I also learned that forgiving my ex was my bridge to God's forgiveness. I learned the truth of Matthew 6:14–15: "For if you forgive men for their transgressions, your heavenly Father will also forgive you. But if you do not forgive men, then your Father will not forgive your transgressions" (NASB).

When exes cannot communicate and bitterness results, it may be one or the other or both at fault. Someone has to begin building bridges, however, and God desires it to be you and me.

At one of our Blended Blessings conferences we encountered Valerie, a divorced single parent who harbored so much bitterness toward her ex-husband that her anger showed in all areas of her appearance. She was the perfect example of the old bumper sticker, "The gods we serve write their names in our faces."

When we discussed the Scriptures regarding forgiving an ex, Valerie did not miss writing one of them down. In the following weeks, it was evident that she was claiming those Scriptures in her life. Her whole appearance began to soften. She developed a radiance and peace that shone from her face. Her appearance was a witness to everyone in her church of the changing power of Christ in her life. Valerie began the process of building this bridge by changing her attitude and being willing to forgive. Remember, we chain ourselves to anyone we refuse to forgive!

Taking Care of Unfinished Business

Another bridge to growth is taking care of unfinished business. All divorces need closure. When there are no children involved, the reasons for contact are removed. This does not, however, eliminate the need for closure so exes can emotionally separate from each other. When this does not happen, we are haunted by memories.

"I was never able to put my mind at rest regarding my former marriage," Robert told us, "until I unexpectedly ran into my ex while working. We visited for a while regarding all that had happened since our divorce. With this conversation, standing in a public place, I was finally able to emotionally bring closure to this relationship. After the visit, however, I was unable to share this experience with my wife, Carrie."

It is not unusual in a blended family to feel reluctant to discuss any positive situation involving our exes. We must be wise and recognize the importance closure plays in freeing ourselves and our mates to go on with current relationships. If there is not emotional closure in the former marriage, there is limited emotional progress in the current marriage. We are not speaking about legal closure—divorce court does that. We are speaking about how much of our present marriage is controlled by our emotional bond to past experiences.

DON: Before LaDean and I married, I had been married for twenty years. In those years, I had built several strong relationships, one of which was with my mother-in-law, Edith. In the years of my marriage with LaDean, I have grown to love her mother, but I have often thought of Edith. Last year my son invited me to the hospital to see Edith, who was dying. Being able to say good-bye to her before she died allowed me to bring closure to that part of my life in more than one way. It also gave me the opportunity to bring closure to the bitterness associated with my feelings for my ex-wife. It was a washing away of the pain and hurt I had carried since the divorce.

LaDean has been so gracious to recognize the importance of this process to our relationship, and the healing has strengthened our love and commitment.

We have realized that having personal peace allows
us to respect our ex-mates, giving them the freedom
to be themselves.

The Respect Factor

The issue of respect is another factor with the potential
to be a barrier or a bridge to personal growth.

Macmillan's Dictionary defines *respect* as "regard for or appreciation of the fundamental worth or value of someone
or something."[1] As we read this definition, our house rule
of common courtesy comes to mind. All persons in our
house value each other. Why would we not expect this rule
to extend outside our home? In our culture, however, it is
common to see ex bashing as an accepted and encouraged
practice.

Often we must force ourselves to extend respect to our
exes. The more we make ourselves do it, however, the more
stable we become within ourselves and in our present relationships. This is not a call to rekindle old flames or to
restore something that has died. We are exercising respect
for basic human dignity. Scripture powerfully commands
us to "do nothing out of selfish ambition or vain conceit,
but in humility consider others better than [ourselves]"
(Philippians 2:3). We are not suggesting that we automatically comply with anything our ex proposes. The more we
overcome our own selfishness and ego, the more we can
respect ourselves. Self-respect is built from confidence in
our value system, which produces confidence in the motives for the decisions we make. Consequently, we can extend respect to our ex-mates. Stability is an outgrowth of
trusting ourselves and our value system so we no longer
live in fear. The result of stability is a feeling of permanence
and direction in life, which gives security.

The Trust Factor

Trust is another bridge- or barrier-building issue. The amount of trust developed will depend on the particular dynamics of each ex couple and the extent to which they allow extended family to influence their relationship. We have found that the more we trust God for our fulfillment and security in life, the easier it is for us to treat our exes with respect.

An important part of trust in dealing with an ex is that the closer we walk with the Lord, the more we depend on him to show us when to use caution or when to pull back. We can treat our exes with respect at all times. We can even discuss issues with them, especially concerning children. There is a point, however, when we sometimes must pull back and say, "I can't deal with that right now; it will have to wait." Our trust in dealing with our exes is not a blind trust, with complete vulnerability, but more of a guarded trust, constantly filtered through our sense of security and what God is doing in each of us right now. Our research tells us that sometimes we feel comfortable trusting an ex in one area, like bringing the children home on time, but don't feel the same level of trust in situations such as financial matters.

The wisdom writing in Proverbs tells us: "Trust in the LORD with all your heart and lean not on your own understanding; in all your ways acknowledge him, and he will make your paths straight" (Proverbs 3:5–6).

Those who have come through emotionally or physically abusive divorces will find it more difficult to develop trust, and rightly so. God does not intend us to continually stay in destructive situations. If our ex-mates are uncooperative or untrustworthy, then we must determine to build a bridge to growth, respect, and trust in our own lives.

Even in the best of circumstances, the relationship with an ex has its limits. The limitations vary depending on the two individuals involved. If either of the two are remarried, it adds another dimension to determining the limits because there are new mates and new families to consider. Sometimes in dealing with these limits we may feel un-Christian because we are not loving "unconditionally." But even Jesus set limits with some people. He died for all, but he did not always give of himself to all people. For example, in Matthew 13:57–58, we are told how Jesus performed few miracles in his hometown of Nazareth because of the people's unbelief. Many times, Jesus and his disciples withdrew to rest from the physical and emotional drain of the needy crowds.

We are setting healthy boundaries for ourselves by saying, "I cannot discuss that issue now; we will have to discuss that another time." We must keep our spiritual and emotional integrity in order to be able to maintain the spirit of Christ.

As our attitudes change, we must realize that our ex-mates may not be growing and changing at the same pace we are. This will require us to be tolerant toward their differences. With God's help, we can gain that tolerance.

Terrible or Tolerant

My marriage did not make it because we were just too different," Adam shared with us during a break at one of our conferences. "What first attracted me to her I came to dislike and then to despise."

What Adam shared is a common problem among couples. We are often attracted to opposites, but what we are attracted to early on may be perceived differently as life progresses.

LADEAN: Long before Don and I met, I attended a divorce recovery class. During one session, I was asked to list the reasons why I felt my divorce had happened. At another session, I listed the reasons I originally married my first husband. I discovered that the same characteristics were on each list. For example, what I first perceived as stability I later perceived as control. What began as gift-giving became control of any clothes I bought after we married. It seemed as if my first husband knew everything and could do anything, while I felt as if I knew nothing. What had changed was my perception of those characteristics and how they related to me.

The Difference Factor

Life would be very boring if we were all alike. Differences are not only necessary for success but are really the fun parts of life God has given us if we can direct our energies toward understanding those differences. If you are divorced and neither you nor your former spouse has yet remarried, this might be a foundation to begin reestablishing a relationship. Our goal in this chapter is not to cause guilt or remorse concerning what we might or might not have done in our marriage, but to give freedom to move on with life rather than continuing to divide our focus.

There is an old saying that we fall in love with and marry strengths, but we go home to live with weaknesses. Most of us are poorly equipped to make a marriage work because we've gotten little or no training. There are no Marriage 101 classes in school, so we mostly learn from our parents. As we grow older, we usually come to the conclusion that our parents did the best they could. We have to take responsibility for our own decisions. They are undeserving of the blame for all our problems.

The Temperament Factor

We are indebted to Florence Littauer for introducing us to the four temperament types and for mentoring us. For futher reading on this subject, see her book *Personality Plus* (Grand Rapids: Revell, 1992).

Hippocrates was an ancient Greek. He saw in people four different modes, temperaments, which he believed were controlled by body fluids. We would not liken our perception of personality to red-hot blood (sanguine), yellow bile (choleric), black bile (melancholy), and phlegm (phlegmatic), but Hippocrates used the body fluids as a vehicle to describe different personality characteristics.

Understanding temperaments frees us to better know ourselves and how we perceive life. This knowledge can help us change our lives. The knowledge of temperaments helps us in our perceptions of other people. This can be liberating in dealing with our exes, even to understanding why we find their personalities irritating!

When we begin to understand another person, we are better able to know when we need to be cautious or assertive, vulnerable or protective, compliant or resistant, tolerant rather than terrible.

Before continuing to read, complete the Preference Indicator at the end of this chapter (pp. 63–64). Follow the directions step-by-step to determine your primary and secondary temperaments. This information will give you new insight into why you act and react like you do.

Recognizing the Temperaments

Now that you have completed the Preference Indicator, you are probably wondering exactly how you can recognize these temperaments. Here is a simple sketch of each one, beginning with the two extroverts, sanguine and choleric, and ending with the two introverts, melancholy and phlegmatic.

Sanguine

Basic Motivation: "Let's have fun."
Character Traits:
- eternal optimist; sees life through rose-colored glasses
- lives in the here and now; enjoys whatever he or she is doing
- decisions are based on feelings rather than logic
- encourages others

Sanguine (Character Traits, *continued*)

- quick to forgive; doesn't always remember what he or she has done; doesn't carry a grudge
- tells good stories but exaggerates details; loves to talk

Body Language:
- demonstrative gestures
- springy "cheerleader" walk
- wears clothing flamboyant in both design and color
- happy-go-lucky
- holds onto other people when talking to them
- wide-open eyes

At one conference we asked a sanguine, "What is the least effective tool you use in dealing with your ex-husband?" She responded, "Communication." For a talkative sanguine, that response spoke volumes. That same woman was asked about the hardest part of working with her ex-husband, and she replied with a sweet smile, "The very thought of it!"

Sanguines suffer depression when the fun is gone. They may not understand the divorce and ask, "Why doesn't my ex want to be with me, being the fun person I am?" However, they will not let themselves feel bad or angry for long. A sanguine who does not have the Lord in his or her life can become a real party animal and may become promiscuous. Sanguines enjoy spending money. In addition, they try to justify their actions. Sanguines might take a poll and use any agreement with their opinions to justify what they are doing. Therefore, they use other people's opinions as their excuse for making the decisions they make.

Choleric

Basic Motivation: "Do it my way, now!"

Character Traits:

- primary goal is accomplishment
- desires productivity over sensitivity
- believes his or her instructions should be followed immediately
- tends to be unsympathetic
- finds it difficult to apologize
- excels in emergencies
- organized, but uses his or her own method of arranging personal possessions
- self-centered, but the most receptive to changing the way he or she thinks, feels, and reacts

Body Language:

- deliberate gestures
- hard heel-toe walk
- stands with weight evenly distributed
- stands with both hands on hips when angry
- when talking, one hand will be on hip while the other is either clenched or has the index finger pointed
- territorial actions
- reacts coolly in emergencies and crises
- often has dramatic, piercing eyes that stare right through you

LADEAN: I like to use the following example to show how cholerics might act and react. "You can go in half with me to buy Trey his computer for graduation," said my ex-husband. "I've already checked with my experts to make sure what he needs." Since Don and I had already thought about buying Trey a computer for graduation and had even discussed the possibility of asking Trey's dad if he wanted to go in on the gift, my first thought was, *Do you know you are speaking to a capital C choleric? You've got this in reverse, buster. You can go in half with me and forget your experts!*

Cholerics do not like to be told what to do; they need to be consulted and given an opportunity to make their own decisions based on their own expert opinions.

Cholerics tend to attack issues mentally and emotionally. They go on a crusade not to allow their emotions to be controlled by any memory of the ex, who is not at all a fun person in their eyes. Each time they are reminded of an ex memory, they might say something like: "I'm not going to think about this anymore. I'm going to think about something else. I don't have any reason to think about this, so I won't."

Cholerics also tend to work their way out of any depressive thoughts by throwing themselves into projects at work or at home. Some of these projects might be clearing out the drawers or the closet the ex used, cleaning the garage, trimming the hedges like the choleric always wanted, throwing away all of the ex's old junk, and moving toiletries to the "good" side of the bathroom cabinet. Cholerics will be the first to decide to get on with life.

Melancholy

Basic Motivation: "If it's worth doing, do it right."
Character Traits:
- perfectionist, including clothing and grooming
- organized
- the most artistic, creative, musical, poetic, and cultured of all the temperaments

Melancholy (Character Traits, *continued*)

- intelligent
- sensitive
- arrives early for appointments because he or she is aware of other people's time
- accurate with facts and figures; good money manager

Body Language:

- stands with weight on one foot with hands clasped in front of self in fig-leaf position
- gestures close to body
- when walking, heel-toes one foot and drags the other heel
- feels more secure if touching an object or leaning against a wall or cabinet with the upper part of the leg
- looks down, thus appears serious
- is depressed over failing personal high standards
- seeks approval

We read in the paper about a man who received a phone call one day that surprised him. His ex-wife of twenty years before called to ask him for a copy of their divorce papers so she could collect on her second husband's Social Security death benefit. She had misplaced her divorce papers years ago. He obliged her and sent a copy so she could fulfill the requirements she needed. Only a serious melancholy would keep divorce papers for his or her whole life.

Melancholies often have the hardest time separating emotionally from their ex-mates. They deal with an issue by analyzing it thoroughly, processing it on their own. They tend to experience depression with an ocean of tears, watching the fog roll in, but then they decide what went wrong and why. They often dwell on everything they themselves did wrong, assuming all the blame.

"If only I had done this or that," or "If I'd just been better or different. How could I have been so dumb?"

Once they have processed the whole situation, they decide they might as well go along with it, because there is nothing else they can do.

Phlegmatic

Basic Motivation: "Don't get too involved. Do it the easy way."

Character Traits:

- easygoing and laid-back; creates and seeks peace
- consistent, secure, comfortable
- normally a background person but will excel in a position of leadership because he or she guides rather than orders
- allows co-workers the freedom to do a job without constant supervision
- great listener but reluctant communicator
- makes friends easily
- good counselor
- accepts others as they are

Body Language:

- stands with weight on one foot and hands in pockets jingling change or with arms crossed over chest
- when sitting, he or she scoots down and crosses his or her arms and legs
- when walking, the person turns his or her feet out and shuffles along

> *Phlegmatic* (Body Language, *continued*)
>
> - watches rather than participates
> - shows little expression
> - holds back on sharing thoughts and feelings
> - will go along with whatever anyone suggests

One phlegmatic in our Sunday school class gave this response to our request for the best thing he had done to deal with his ex.

"I'll tell you the most wonderful story you ever heard," he deadpanned in a low, slow drawl. "I haven't seen or spoken to her in four years."

Phlegmatics depend on events to motivate them to emotionally sever the ties. Some contact with their exes will cause them to turn loose. Then any effort to change their opinions will meet with a quiet will of iron. Phlegmatics tend to be depressed, and it's an immobilizing depression, causing them to be couch potatoes. Their loved ones may become worried about their inability to get on with life. When phlegmatics are ready, they will use an incident with their exes as motivation to quietly go about resuming life.

The Blend Factor

As we begin to understand the differences in the four temperaments, we can look at how they blend together. We are primarily one and secondarily another temperament. It is not unusual to possess one or two qualities of the other two temperaments.

The two natural blends are the sanguine-choleric and the melancholy-phlegmatic. It doesn't matter which temperament is primary or secondary, the blend is still the same. The sanguine-choleric is optimistic, outgoing, and outspoken. The melancholy-phlegmatic is analytical, pessimistic, and soft-spoken. The two temperaments in each of these blends have more characteristics that are alike than are different.

The two complimentary blends are the choleric-melancholy and the sanguine-phlegmatic. The two temperaments in each of these blends have some characteristics that are similar but also some characteristics that are very different, and these differences can cause inner conflict in some people.

The choleric-melancholy is the work blend. These people want to do the job and do it right. They tend to be decisive, organized, and goal-oriented. On the other hand, their emotional needs are very different. Melancholies cry when they are happy or sad. They cry when they're glad and they cry when they're mad. They cry when things are good, and they cry when things are bad. However, all these tears are a real trauma for a front-running choleric, who thinks that tears are a sign of weakness, so there may be some real inner conflict.

The sanguine-phlegmatic is the play blend. These people want to do the job the easiest, most fun way. They are witty and easygoing rather than goal-oriented. Inner conflict arises because sanguines thrive on relationships, but phlegmatics don't want too much involvement. Those who have this blend enjoy solitude until they realize they're not having fun. The sanguine wants to go do something, but the phlegmatic wants to sit comfortably and regroup.

The Application Factor

Understanding our ex-mate's temperament can help us deal more effectively with him or her. There are some basic principles to remember in dealing with our exes. The first principle is: Being different is not being wrong; it is just being different. It is not our job to change others, only to understand them. We must extend to others, and that includes our exes, the same consideration we expect others to extend to us. We need to let people be themselves.

A second principle is: Any strength carried to an extreme becomes a weakness. The opposite is true also—any weakness can be polished up and can become a strength. This principle can be very important when used for personal introspection. And, as we begin to work on making ourselves more understanding, we may be amazed to find that we perceive our exes in ways that make our interaction more positive.

It is not our job to change others, only to understand them.

One of the first things we must decide is what kind of relationship we want with an ex. This is a strange, awkward situation even when the divorce has been harmonious. We may not get the relationship we want, but we might get the opportunity to grow through the relationship we have. We, who at one time pledged our love to each other, have now severed the legal relationship. There must be a turning loose time that involves our emotions, and each temperament works through this differently.

Once we have a handle on our own temperaments, we can have more success in dealing with an ex by working into his or her temperament rather than out of our own. For example, if your ex is a choleric, you would address their need for power by carefully choosing what they control. Keep in mind that whatever blend your ex is requires you to consider the characteristics of both temperaments when dealing with them. God would have us be conciliatory. A challenging verse in Scripture is: "Make every effort to live in peace with all men and to be holy; without holiness no one will see the Lord" (Hebrews 12:14). This gets right to the heart of what it takes to please God in our relationships. We must not harbor hatred and bitterness. The Bible does not tell us we can never be angry. It does tell us: "Keep away from angry, short-tempered men, lest you learn to be like them and endanger your soul" (Proverbs 22:24–25 TLB). The following chart offers brief, but not exhaustive suggestions for working into our ex's temperament.

Working into My Ex's Temperament

	Sanguine	Choleric	Melancholy	Phlegmatic
Do	Appreciate their humor Make communication as pleasant as possible	Be clear, logical, and succinct—cut to the chase	Have facts together and detailed	Suggest and allow time for them to act
Don't	Criticize Try to make them sad Make fun of Make them feel stupid	Challenge and give ultimatums Argue with Let them run over you	Be flighty, unorganized, or mean Remind them of the past	Force issues of time and decision
Conversation Starters	"You will see how to make the solution pleasant for all of us. Please consider my thoughts."	"Your opinion is important to a solution we can both live with. Here are some ideas I have on the issue."	"You will be able to draw up a perfect plan for us. I would like to share some feelings in the matter."	"You will know the least stressful way to solve the problem. Could I make some suggestions?"

Remember, we are responsible for 100 percent of our actions. If our exes decide not to cooperate at all in whatever relationships we have, then we are still 100 percent ac-

countable for our attitudes and behaviors, realizing we can't
control or choreograph how other people act.

Harmony in relationships is a cycle that feeds itself, so
that the more we seek harmony with others, the more our
inner selves are harmonious. Sometimes we have to be very
creative in order to avoid conflict.

Preference Indicator

easily distracted	not time conscious	easily angered	selectively organized
promoter	impulsive	confrontive	impatient
emotional	entertainer	director	decisive
spontaneous	optimistic	get it done	believable
charming	hands-on	determined	outspoken
energetic	erratic	competitive	challenges
panicky	keep it simple	take charge	aggressive
bubbly	sunshine	initiator	take control
silly	forgetful	pursuing	task-motivated
funny	fit in	opinionated	tough-minded
witty	blend in	planner	analytical
coordinator	indecisive	moody	accurate
even tempered	diplomatic	respectful	scheduled
procrastinator	obliging	organizer	cautious
adaptable	compliant	long lasting	structured
steady	easygoing	exact	deep thinker
listener	contemplative	sensitive to others	sympathetic
calm	tentative	correct	easily depressed
people watcher	observant	conservative	not forgetful
harmonious	like to delegate	tenderhearted	serious

Instructions

Circle any words in the Preference Indicator that characterize your personality most of the time.

After you have circled on the chart the words that characterize you:

1. Draw a vertical line in the space in the middle of the Preference Indicator.
2. Draw a horizontal line in the space in the middle of the Preference Indicator.
3. Beginning in the upper left-hand corner and moving clockwise, label each square as S, C, M, and P. Your sheet should look like this:

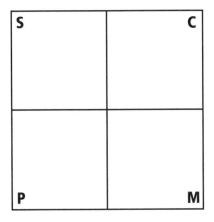

4. Total the number of circled words in each square and write the total here, in the corresponding square.

- The highest total is your primary temperament.
- The second highest total is your secondary temperament.

Conflict or Creativity

B utch and Rita had taken his daughter, Jenny, camping for the weekend. They arrived home late for Jenny's agreed-upon return to Lynn, Butch's ex. Butch typically returned his daughter on time, but this trip had complications that resulted in his family being late. Rita insisted that Jenny take a shower before she go home. Lynn, irritated because Butch was late, came to the house to collect her daughter. She stormed up the steps onto the front porch and demanded that Jenny come outside and get in the car. At the same time, Rita was in the house instructing Jenny to get in the shower. Butch definitely had a "power-mates" struggle, which had become a common occurrence.

"I was in the doorway with our daughter," Butch told us. "Both women were screaming instructions to me to relay to the other one. I was wishing that my daughter and I could just evaporate and whisk off to some peaceful place."

As Butch painted this picture of being caught between his ex-wife and his wife, we asked, "Butch, what did you finally do to solve this dilemma?"

"You know, I don't even remember what the solution was. I just know we all were alive when it was over."

The Conflict Factor

Many exes live out this scenario every week. Being unable to remember how we worked through highly stressful situations is common. Often the stress level in a confrontation is so high the details are lost in the emotion of the situation. Constant conflict in one area of life often leads to underlying anger and hostility in every relationship.

Hostility is not automatic; it can be controlled. Overreaction often triggers anger, and anger can escalate into rage very easily. We can also underreact, deny our feelings, and discredit the situation. This usually makes our exes angry. Then, they may keep our kids from seeing us, and we may then lash out at the people nearest us, our present family. Overreaction and underreaction both create hostility.

Society also fosters within us feelings of hostility toward former mates and toward "step-mates" (the former mate of the present spouse). It is the wicked-step-mother syndrome.

Getting rid of these hostilities requires change, commitment, and communication where exes are involved. Jesus told his followers: "You have heard that it was said, 'You shall love your neighbor, and hate your enemy.' But I say to you, love your enemies, and pray for those who persecute you in order that you may be sons of your Father who is in heaven; for He causes His sun to rise on the evil and the good, and sends rain on the righteous and the unrighteous" (Matthew 5:43–45 NASB).

This does not mean there will never be any more disagreements. We can only take care of our part of the conflict. But we can make sure that what we say and do does not contribute to our ex's part of the conflict. We must become more a part of the solution for conflict—not a source of irritation.

The Creative Factor

Creativity would not be necessary if we always called the shots or controlled every situation. However, when we deal with exes, we know we do not always dictate. We must creatively spark our imaginations to create appropriate methods of dealing with them that are different than the ones we have been using. This does not necessarily mean totally new concepts but innovative ways to get to the desired result.

An important principle to keep in mind is that we must always be creative and not allow ourselves to be locked into just one way of dealing with others, especially our ex-mates.

Butch had to learn to deal with the conflict between his ex and his wife in a creative way. Since every situation is unique, there are no hard-and-fast rules. Adjustments have to be made continually when what we are doing is not working. Sometimes we have to keep trying new approaches until we find something that works.

Butch's creativity began within himself. He became more assertive based on his confidence in and his commitment to his present marriage. He told Rita she had to deal directly with his ex-wife regarding any problems between the two of them, thus removing himself from the "tug-of-war" game. He realized all the adults were in a learning and growing situation, and as he allowed time to heal old wounds, the stress level was reduced. The stress had been fed, in part, by competition between the two women over Butch's loyalty and attention. Another factor feeding the stress was that Lynn, the ex-wife, may have felt her relationship with her daughter was being threatened as Jenny became attached to her stepmother.

In addition, Butch often confronted Rita rather than confronting his ex-wife. This is not unusual. Many noncustodial parents hesitate to confront their exes, fearing the possible loss of visitation time with their children.

An important principle to keep in mind is that we must always be creative and not allow ourselves to be locked into just one way of dealing with others, especially our ex-mates. What works in one situation may not be successful the next time.

Resolving conflict boils down to three "basic Be's."

Be assertive—Butch was assertive when he began communicating openly with Rita about her responsibility in dealing directly with Lynn. He made it clear that the two women must deal with any differences between the two of them.

Be patient—Butch was patient by allowing time to heal some wounds.

Be flexible—Butch realized that what worked one time might need to be adjusted the next time difficulty arises. Sometimes Butch might have to take a more active role in the "power-mate" struggle.

These Be's need to be applied in every situation in dealing with our ex-mates. How often we employ each Be will be determined by the needs or demands of a particular situation. We begin by changing our perception, committing to work on the relationship, and improving our communication skills.

The Change Factor

The changes we need to make have to do with our perceptions of our exes in relation to how much contact we have with them. When children are involved issues such as child support, visitation, weddings, graduations, and funerals require us to be business partners. We may not necessarily admire or respect some business associates, but we maintain appropriate contacts in order to have success.

The cost of not being willing to change perceptions and deal from a business perspective is that we may have a Pyrrhic victory—a battle won at such a high cost that we lose the war. For example, we may feel we have won the battle for the children using hate and anger, only to see our adult children living with a void in their lives because of the loss of relationship with one parent. In reality, both parents lose.

Changing Our Commitment

Whether children are involved or not, we must break the chains of the old relationship. This requires a change in perception so that we don't compare each new person we meet to the former spouse.

Part of the change in perception is how we perceive commitment. Divorce terminated the commitment to the ex. Now, we must determine to what we are willing to commit and what the depth of commitment will be.

We are not recommitting to our exes, but we are challenging ourselves to find workable solutions to whatever situations the two of us are dealing with. Women, for example, are not expected to submit to their ex-husbands. They become equals in whatever decisions must be made.

We must also be committed to our own integrity. As we successfully deal with feelings and rebuild self-esteem, we will be emotionally and spiritually strong enough to stand up for what we know is just and right. We also will be flexible without being walked on. It takes strong resolve to back away from any efforts by our exes to gain control of our self-images, but we can do it a statement at a time, perhaps saying something like: "I'm sorry; I cannot respond to you when you speak to me in this way. I am willing to discuss this again at another time."

Our unwillingness to be manipulated or humiliated may surprise or disappoint our exes, but these kinds of statements are evidence that we are willing to discuss issues.

Changing Our Communication

In the beginning, most communication with an ex is not a social function; it is business of some sort, usually dealing with the kids' situations. There is no need for fluffy, frivolous chatter. The direct approach may be needed. It may be advantageous to have an agenda for these discussions.

More positive results will happen when we listen more than we talk. We can never think of this statement without remembering Don's mother saying, "Remember, God gave you two ears and one mouth. He expects you to listen twice as much as you talk."

We must express our desires without being demanding. Leave nothing to guesswork or memory; ask for clarification, and then write it down. Never forget that this relationship is one with limitations.

We must keep in mind that there are people who are bound and determined to sabotage whatever they think their ex-mates want to happen. When someone is in a destructive pattern in life, it is very important not to give fuel to that fire. We may need to choose not to be involved in an ex's destructive cycle. This may mean we hang up the phone or walk away. No good is accomplished through destructive communication. This does not mean that we have no contact with an ex, but we must remove ourselves from being a party to his or her anger.

The Phone Tone

Gary Smalley and John Trent note that "Communication experts tell us that words comprise only about 7% of communication. Body language is 55%, and tone of voice is 38%."[1] With these statistics in mind, the phone becomes a very good tool for talking with our exes. On the phone, our exes are not able to see our body language and, therefore, cannot react to it. We have time to regroup before we say anything, so that we can control our words and our tone of voice. Another plus is that the emotional level can be more easily controlled. If our exes become irrational in the conversation, we can simply say: "I'm sorry, I cannot talk further like this. I am hanging up now."

LADEAN: I mildly reprimanded my ex in a recent conversation. As I was confronting him about a situation, he quickly brought the conversation to a close. As I hung up the phone, I broke into laughter and thought, *You know, that is one nice thing about being divorced. When you don't want to listen anymore, you simply find a reason to get off the phone. You don't have to talk about it.*

Remember, we need to be careful what we say and how we say it. Our exes could be taping our conversations. This is another reason to take some time in responding to an ex. The result of being careful in what we say is good for both parties, since communication will be more accurate and concise.

The Ambush

One of the toughest situations to deal with when communicating with an ex is to have an "ambush" topic brought up. An ambush topic is an issue not related to the subject with which we are dealing, brought up to manipulate and control the emotion of the moment. Ambushing handicaps the person not prepared to talk about the subject. When our exes want to get their way and the harmony of the conversation has been destroyed, they feel justified in saying: "I just can't talk to you! All we do is fight. That is why we are not married anymore."

One creative way to reduce the damage of this situation is to be tough enough to calmly respond: "I'm sorry, I can't talk about this right now. I'll be glad to discuss it on Monday at 7:00 P.M."

LADEAN: I repeated that very statement six times in a conversation with my ex one night while discussing our son. That conversation was the beginning of a foundation of peace that allowed Trey to be raised without conflict between his parents. Those healthy connections were based on clearly defined guidelines and honesty. They have lasted because my ex-husband and I have been willing to continue investing in the process even with its limitations. It is more of a surface relationship, but the surface is secure by making sure that the issues discussed are clearly defined, agreed-upon (as best we can), and are as few as necessary.

It is always acceptable to retreat when we feel ourselves being drawn into a web of confusion. When having trouble making a decision with our exes, a good rule is to allow some time until I am ready to make the decision. Remember, "God is not a God of disorder but of peace" (1 Corinthians 14:33).

A Go-Between

Some of us may need to use a mediator or go-between when communication is impossible with our exes. The go-between could be a lawyer, a professional mediator, or a person agreed upon as acceptable to both parties. The go-between *cannot be any of our children!* Children must not be put in the position of communicating between adults. We read of one little girl who finally said to her dad: "Daddy, when you and Mommy yell and scream at each other, I'm not able to talk loud enough for you to hear me. I can't do this anymore; you'll have to find someone else."

Through interviews with several professional mediators, we determined there are both advantages and disadvantages to mediation, as follows:

Advantages of Mediation

Keeps you from going back to court, which is both expensive and public

Does not require an attorney

Allows venting of hurt feelings, which sometimes brings closure

Is voluntary—the two individuals who have sought mediation make the decisions

Creates an atmosphere that allows ex-mates to discuss their individual needs and to resolve conflicts

Disadvantages of Mediation

Gives suggestions, not orders—if you need to be told what to do, you may be frustrated

Does not provide legal advice

Does not require parties to be legally bound to the agreement—individuals can back out or change their minds

Will not work for you if you are interested in fighting for your rights or in hurting the other person

Because mediation is based on resolution of conflict, it begins constructive communication between the ex-mates.

Constructive Not Destructive

Communication needs to be constructive rather than destructive. In their book, *Leaving the Light On*, Trent and Smalley say, "Words have the awesome power to build us up or tear us down emotionally."[2] We begin building constructive communication by choosing our words carefully, words that build up rather than tear down. Choosing our words carefully must be tied to controlling our emotions and focusing on the discussion at hand.

LADEAN: We had an engagement party for my son and his fiancée, Sarah, at our home. Even though I had given George, my ex-husband, all the party details, he called and asked, "You don't have much room at your house; do you want to use the fellowship hall at my church?" I sweetly replied, "No, I'm going to have it in our home." Had I allowed emotions about the past to rule my reply, I would have launched on a path of destruction. George's motives were probably the best, but without my restraint, those motives would have been buried in the rubble. I have learned to take deep breaths and gather myself while waiting to give my reply. This is my way of counting to ten. I have tried to follow Jesus' instruction: "Simply let your 'Yes' be 'Yes,' and your 'No,' 'No'" (Matthew 5:37).

We have to learn more than one creative way to communicate with our exes. Nearly all people who are exes got that way because of poor communication. Some of us do not know how to communicate effectively. Our (Don and LaDean's) counselor, Brooke Annis, once told us we were like parrots; both of us talked but neither of us listened. We began to study communication and to put our newfound knowledge to work. Brooke taught us to take what we were saying to each other at face value, without judgment. The same principle can help us deal with our exes. We can learn to take what our ex-mates communicate at face value, while understanding that the relationship has its limits.

Being creative in the way we avoid conflict is brain work. We have to consciously think of new ways to approach our exes inoffensively. When we are in crises, we must come up with new, nonthreatening ways to approach situations. Oops! It sounds a little like manipulation, doesn't it? Maybe it is, but it is directed toward a positive solution.

Changing our commitment and our communication is critical when establishing some type of acceptable working relationship with our exes. This process is a cycle—sometimes things seem to go well, and then we hit a pothole in the relationship. Often, there doesn't seem to be any apparent reason; it just happens. We must remain consistent in our own behaviors and not react to others' ups and downs. We are seeing more people willing to build a working relationship with their former mates, so have hope—it *can* be done.

Bitter or Better

I feel like a nervous wreck," Jamie said to her daughter Donna as they arrived at the airport. This was their first big trip together since Jamie's divorce. Jamie had tried to make sure nothing was forgotten. She had checked and double-checked their luggage and passports. She even had the letter from her ex-husband giving Donna permission to leave the country (they were headed to Saint Thomas). Jamie remembered telling Charles the letter had to be exactly as directed by law, but he had said, "This will do." At this point, she certainly hoped so.

Jamie opened her wallet at the gate.

"Oh no!" she cried. "I forgot to pick up my driver's license on the table at home."

Jamie's sister offered to go get it since Jamie had to have this form of ID to make the trip. Her sister made it in time, but meanwhile the airline personnel told Jamie that Charles's letter was not in the correct form for Donna to leave the country.

Jamie picked up the phone and called her ex-husband, who was now remarried. His new wife, and former secretary, answered the phone. Jamie asked to speak to Charles.

"I'm sorry, but he's asleep."

"Obviously, you did not understand what I said. Let me speak to Charles!"

"But he's sleeping," said the small voice.

"Please listen carefully. If you do not wake him up and let me talk to him now, you will see a major miracle. I will come through this phone line and wrap it around your neck. Do you understand!"

"Just a moment," whispered the small voice.

"Hello, what do you want?" Charles asked gruffly.

"Charles, remember that letter you said would be good enough? Well, it's not! Donna and I are at the airport, and they are holding the charter for us. If you don't get here immediately, you will pay for the fifteen-hundred-dollar tickets, and then I'll let you explain to your daughter why this happened."

There was a pause.

"I'll be right there."

Jamie and Donna finally boarded the plane to a thunderous cheer and a standing ovation from the passengers.

"I thought the passengers were cheering because we had at last gotten on the plane," Jamie told us. "We learned, during the flight, people had also cheered because I actually got an ex-mate to do something!"

Jamie had been working hard to be polite anytime she talked to her ex, but this situation called for a more assertive stance. While she might have been kinder to her ex's new wife, she realized she must put some order back into her life by taking charge. For years she had felt like a victim, and she knew that had to change. Her decision to be civil was part of her bridge from bitter to better. She made a conscious decision to live in life's humor rather than in sadness. In stressful situations, it may help to repeat the philosophy, "This time next year we'll laugh!" When dealing with our ex-mates, we often must laugh or we end up crying or becoming bitter.

How do we deal with bitterness? Do we allow life to make us bitter or better? Ask yourself, Who catches the brunt of my frustration, anger, or feelings of helplessness?

Humor—The Number One Release from Bitterness

Anyone who has an ex-mate can appreciate Jamie's story. The more she talked, at one of our conferences in California, the more laughter there was, until all of us were nearly rolling on the floor. Jamie had learned to use laughter and humor as a release from bitterness.

In our book *Remarried with Children,* we note the following:

> The ability to laugh with others rather than at them and to laugh at yourself is critical to health and wellness. In fact, the positive effects of humor on our bodies have received increasing attention from medical researchers. Some hospitals have created "humor rooms." Sometimes a sense of humor can be the vehicle to help you relax, to have the freedom to go on living. I don't believe God wants us to handle everything with a joke, but when circumstances are completely out of your control, a laugh can be your statement that anger and bitterness are not going to rule your life. This can give you the courage to let God control the situation. The ability to laugh at your circumstances and at your future will help you establish relationships, relieve anxiety, reduce stress, release anger, and facilitate learning.[1]

Keeping Anger in Check

Bitterness is anger left unchecked. Self-evaluation helps us keep our own actions and responses in perspective. We must evaluate each situation as a separate entity. In this way we start with a clean slate each time we have to deal with our exes. It takes self-evaluation and work on our part not to have a carryover effect from each incident. Not allowing ourselves to store up wrongs makes our lives better, not bitter.

Bitterness is built on a foundation of outside circumstances, almost all of which cannot be changed. What can be changed is how we perceive these circumstances and how we react to them. We must take control of what we allow these circumstances to do to and in us.

Am I Angry with My Ex?

A friend of ours once said, "When people get divorced, men get sad and women get mad." We don't know that the genders are always the same in this, but often someone is sad, and someone is mad.

Paul tells us in Ephesians: "If you are angry, don't sin by nursing your grudge. Don't let the sun go down with you still angry—get over it quickly" (Ephesians 4:26 TLB). We do not lose our emotions when we accept Christ as our Savior and Lord, but our emotions are purified as we submit them to the direction of the Holy Spirit.

> *Not allowing ourselves to store up wrongs makes our lives better, not bitter.*

Are we unhappy with our exes because *we* are so unhappy on the inside that anything they do makes us angry? Or, are we unhappy with our exes because *their* behavior sometimes causes unhappiness in our lives? All of us admit we periodically get angry; however, few of us admit we are angry people. We most often don't know how to deal with this anger.

If we never like anything our exes do, if we are continually disappointed in them, if nothing they do is ever good enough, we are probably filtering all of life's experiences through an underlying anger. We may like to think this only shows in our dealings with our exes, but anger surfaces in every area of our lives—our jobs, our relationships, and more. Therefore, there is no peace.

LADEAN: My anger followed me everywhere. When I felt happy, I would subconsciously find something that irritated me so I could express my hostility. One Sunday at church, I began to realize I was angry when I heard a message I felt was intended for me.

In his sermon, Charles Clary, pastor of Tate Springs Baptist Church in Arlington, Texas, explained that anger has five levels. It begins with *irritation*, or being bothered by something, and progresses to *indignation*, realizing that a wrong has been done. Next comes *wrath*, reactions such as throwing something or kicking the dog. The next level is *fury*, which is brutal and vengeful. We begin to feel beside ourselves, which may lead to violence. The final stage is *rage*. Now we have totally lost control and may not even remember afterward the violent things we have done.

I found myself at the irritation and indignation levels, and I would occasionally progress to wrath, where I might even slam the cabinet or the bathroom door. The continual presence of these three levels of anger robbed me and my loved ones of true joy. Anyone who has been in an abusive situation has witnessed these levels of anger and knows how quickly an innocent situation can become distorted to the point of wrath, fury, or even rage. Whether we are the person with the anger or we were married to the person with abusive anger or if our child has this anger, it is a most frightening experience.

Now, whenever I feel angry, I remind myself of two verses of Scripture: "Have you any right to be angry?"

(Jonah 4:4), and "Do not be angry beyond measure, O LORD; do not remember our sins forever" (Isaiah 64:9).

After remembering these Scriptures, I ask myself two questions: "Do I have reason to be angry? Is my anger out of proportion to the offense?"

Praise God for choreographing my presence at that Sunday morning service, for what I've learned about temperaments, and for counseling that has led me to a love affair with the Lord that brings inner peace. This is not to say I don't experience irritation or periods of indignation, but I do not feel the wrath I once felt.

Am I Angry with God?

God created us with a free will that allows us to make choices. He doesn't make us choose in a certain way, but he will direct us when we ask and are willing to follow. When we make poor choices, God still loves us and desires our greatest joy. However, the consequences of our choices can alter our lives.

Divorce, like death, leaves us feeling empty in that a relationship has died. Several people we interviewed confessed to times of being angry at God—over the divorce, the family breakup, the loss of stability, and a feeling of helpless abandonment. When people become angry at God, they blame him. If you find yourself here, realize the anger is yours and God did not cause your divorce.

Although most people experience anger associated with a divorce, not everyone directs their anger at God. In their despair they often find themselves drawn to God. This offers the opportunity to seek stability and love in him. You can throw yourself on his mercy and grace and find both gifts there.

Unresolved anger often comes with a critical spirit. But when we have inner peace, even the anger we sometimes feel is filtered through the peace. Inner peace is an unmistakable ability to find the joy in each moment.

Resolving Anger

Anger is a reality in the world in which we live. What we do about it makes the difference. There is a difference in being angry and in being an angry person. Mary shared her story with us.

Mary was a sheltered young Christian woman who had married a young man going to school to be a pastor, but now she was divorced. She had been battered by her husband for several years before she was convinced it was OK for her to leave. The situation had not been getting better; in fact, the violence was escalating.

After the divorce, she dealt with the issues of her Christian responsibility in the situation. She kept asking herself the same questions: *Was it all my fault? Was I not submissive enough? Did I not meet his needs? Could I have loved him more or in a better way? How can I be a Christian and be in this predicament?*

Her guilt was magnified by the fact that some of her friends and a Christian counselor had advised her to stay in the marriage and pray for God to change her husband. She felt as if she had betrayed God. These kinds of issues attacked her at the core of her self-esteem, and she fought depression, anger, and bitterness. She saw only failure in everything important in her life.

After several fruitless efforts to discuss reconciliation with her ex-husband, Mary made up her mind she was not going to live a life full of anger and hate. She did feel anger at her ex, at herself, and at life for all she had gone through. However, she knew her future happiness, whatever it might be, was dependent on her attitude about all these questions and feelings.

Mary immersed herself in seeking God's forgiveness and his will for her. She submerged herself in the Scriptures, seeking answers to the questions with which she was struggling. She began to find those answers, one by one, and she dealt with them as they emerged. She claimed the truth of the Scriptures, whether it was a promise, assurance, or a confirmation of her decisions. She lived by those principles, and she fought off the old destructive feelings using God's Word. Only then did she experience God's joy!

We use four steps for resolving anger. As Mary retraced her anger, she realized she could find herself in each step.

1. *Recognize it.* Recognition of anger is threefold. We must first see that we are angry. If you found yourself anywhere in Mary's story, then you must admit, "Tag; I'm it." The second step in recognition is to accept responsibility for your anger. It is not our exes or our kids or our spouses who make us mad. Anger is our response to what others have done. The last step in recognition is to see what happened to cause our anger. This part of recognition may take a while, and we may need some help to get there.

With the help of our pastor, Dr. David George, we came up with seven causes of anger. We become angry: (1) when we are not taken seriously; (2) when we are rejected; (3) when we are hurt; (4) when we are made to feel small or unimportant; (5) when we feel pressured to do things we don't want to do; (6) when we feel we are not in control of our lives; (7) when decisions that affect us are made without our input.

DON: After LaDean and I married, I began seeking God, and he brought some special people into my life to help me see my anger. Lana Bateman, founder of Philippian Ministries, showed me where my anger was com-

ing from. Then it was up to me to ask God to give me
the strength to make the changes needed in my life.

2. *Release it.* Releasing anger requires that we do four
things. First, we must release what is not eternally important because we no longer have to make anyone pay. Second, we claim the prayer of Saint Francis of Assisi and accept those things we cannot change as we change those
things we can. Having the wisdom to know the difference
is what this process is all about. Third, we release what happened to us, real or imagined. There are other things in our
lives that are more important to us now. Finally, we forgive
anyone involved, living or not. Forgiving without working
through our anger produces an incomplete result.

3. *Recover from it.*

DON: My recovery came with determination. I began recov-
         ering by refusing to allow anger about the past to con-
         trol my attitude and actions. Every time these thoughts
         came to my mind, I had to visualize putting them in a
         trash can and putting the lid on it. I continued by fill-
         ing my life with what is positive and by allowing the
         experiences I've had to soften rather than to harden
         my heart. Positive influences can include music, books,
         Scripture, and friends. I found it necessary to seek pro-
         fessional help from a counselor.

Other sources of professional help are pastors or other
church staff, lawyers, or psychologists.

4. *Rejoice in freedom from it.* Knowing God personally
gives inner peace, and we can live more relaxed lives, without fighting and striving. We celebrate freedom from the
bonds of anger by living in joy each day, refusing to be critical and judgmental, smiling at life's new adventures, and

losing our "worry buttons"—the "what ifs" and "maybes" that cause worry when pushed by ourselves or others. We lose them by reacting in reality and not in worry. We can now "Rejoice in the Lord always" (Philippians 4:4).

Keeping Criticism in Check

Mary was criticized by her friends for not being willing to stay in the abusive relationship and for not trusting God to change her husband. Sadly, sometimes the strongest criticism comes from family and friends. Grandparents, when children are involved, can put pressure on parents to stay in a marriage. They often fear the loss of contact with their grandchildren or the stigma of having a divorced person in their family. And children and in-laws are often the most severe critics.

One of the hardest issues to deal with concerning criticism is understanding that family and friends really do mean well. We may know this at an intellectual level, but at a feeling level we still can be irritated by constant reminders of what we have or haven't done.

LADEAN: An important relationship was impaired when I responded to a well-meaning friend's advice. After many conversations where my friend Ila emphasized the importance of keeping our family together, I remember saying to her, "If you are having trouble deciding whose friend to be, just be his!"

She did not quit being my friend, but we did put distance between us. It has taken fifteen years for us to begin repairing the relationship we once had. However, through all of this, God has used friends and events as the threads that kept us in contact with each other.

When our ex-mates criticize us, we tend to become more critical of and angrier toward them. It is hard not to talk negatively about those who have hurt us, especially our ex-mates. Yet God's Word commands us: "Don't criticize and speak evil about each other, dear brothers. If you do, you will be fighting against God's law of loving one another, declaring it is wrong. But your job is not to decide whether this law is right or wrong, but to obey it" (James 4:11 TLB).

James encourages us to refrain from faultfinding, yet we are to learn from constructive criticism: "If you profit from constructive criticism, you will be elected to the wise men's hall of fame. But to reject criticism is to harm yourself and your own best interests" (Proverbs 15:31–32 TLB).

Even though these principles go against our human nature, we must intentionally practice the truths in these two Scriptures. Having self-control will bring peace to our lives.

Stuffing Criticism

When faced with criticism, some people become negative and critical. Others of us suppress, or stuff, our feelings. While it's true that we must put our feelings behind us, it doesn't necessarily mean that we should deny or ignore them. Here is a better use for the word *stuff*. The next time you are tempted to explode in anger or to swallow your feelings, try using the following acrostic:

Search yourself and see if the criticism applies to you.

Treat the situation by immersing yourself in the Scriptures.

Unmask your pride so you can deal with your attitudes or actions.

Face the situation or person without an explosion.

Forget undue criticism; go on with life, leaving the muck behind.

Paul instructed us to look to the future: "No, dear brothers, I am still not all I should be but I am bringing all my energies to bear on this one thing: Forgetting the past and looking forward to what lies ahead, I strain to reach the end of the race and receive the prize for which God is calling us up to heaven because of what Christ Jesus did for us" (Philippians 3:13–14 TLB).

Is your external focus on your internal problems, or is your internal focus on your external problems? In this chapter we have focused on internal issues resulting in bitterness. In the next chapter we are going to look at our external situations through different eyes.

Warfare or "Well-fare"

As he left the courthouse, Sam remarked to his friend Doug, "I feel as if my life has been reduced to a piece of paper. From now on until the kids are eighteen, I'll be living by that divorce decree. You know what's odd? With a rap of the gavel, all the years Susie and I were together have been done away with. Here I am, thirty-five years old, and I feel as if I gave her all the best years of my life. Susie and I didn't agree on much, but the few things we did agree on beforehand the judge changed."

These are common sentiments heard after divorce court. The things we feel we have lost are hard to put in a divorce document. Children's affections, self-esteem, money and possessions, status in the community, long-term friendships, church family—all are areas of our lives affected by the courtroom decisions. Keep in mind that both parties usually leave the court feeling as if they lost. The courtroom draws the battle lines of warfare from that point forward. Until we overcome these feelings of loss, anytime we deal with our exes we try to reclaim what we felt we lost in the courtroom.

Most warfare between exes surfaces when issues involving the children arise. The real warfare below the surface is unresolved anger and hostility between the two adults, resulting from their sense of loss.

Divided Loyalties

Part of the unfairness of divorce situations is that they do not involve just the two ex-mates. Often, there is a new mate and sometimes a new family on both sides. Divided loyalties between the original family and the new family result in conflicts of time, energy, and money. When we are in a power struggle with our exes, we tend to bring that stress into our new families, so warfare erupts there also. If our exes sense the tension and stress taking place in our new families, they may try to create new problems for us. In addition, when our children are having difficulty finding their niche in either family, all this confusion and frustration provides an opportunity for them to direct more pressure toward the parents. This kind of chaos is one reason so many divorced people struggle with staying remarried.

"A gentle answer turns away wrath, but a harsh word stirs up anger" (Proverbs 15:1). In the heat of frustration, claiming this Scripture allows us to stay in a state of "well-fare" rather than warfare. Instead of shaming our exes or losing our self-control, we can address what is best for us and for our children in the situation.

Often we hear from couples that the new wife in a second marriage does not feel her husband is firm enough with his ex-wife. A new mate can become angry because there are two standards of tolerance. What is accepted and tolerated in one family unit differs greatly from what is accepted and tolerated in the other family unit. The new mate often feels he or she is having to live by a more strict standard of behavior than is expected of the ex. Those kinds of feelings will always result in conflict. For example, if a husband allows himself to be bullied by his ex-wife, he may try to establish an authoritarian relationship where he feels more confident—with his new wife—and she will probably resist.

When an Ex Controls Our New Home

When we let our exes control what goes on in our new homes, we have invited them to be part of our new families. Therefore, we have "ex-habitation." Our reactions to what our exes do determine how much ex-habitation takes place.

For example, one ex-husband delayed his child-support check whenever he was short of funds. By the time the child-support agency contacted him, he would deposit money in the bank to cover it. This shrewd maneuver was devastating to his ex-wife, who depended on receiving his check at a certain time each month. She was often put in the position of not being able to pay her bills on time, as well as of depriving her children of essentials. The same problem occurs when a child-support check bounces.

In cases like these, the ex-wife has several options. She can take her ex-husband to court, which costs both spouses more money, time, and aggravation. In this option, she may become furious each time her ex's check is delayed, and her new family reaps that anger and frustration. She must be careful not to involve the children in "Daddy sabotage." Her other option, the one most commonly chosen, is to live with her ex's negligence and make the adjustments within her budget and with her creditors. The only real control she has is not to let the matter affect her inner peace. A good Scripture passage to claim is: "Finally, all of you, live in harmony with one another; be sympathetic, love as brothers, be compassionate and humble. Do not repay evil with evil or insult with insult, but with blessing, because to this you were called so that you may inherit a blessing" (1 Peter 3:8–9).

The pressure caused by ex-habitation creates additional confusion for a Christian woman who is struggling with submission to a second husband. She may see her new husband exhibiting a very submissive role in relation to his ex-wife, while expecting her to be very submissive to him. This scenario can be incredibly frustrating. Not only will she rebel, but the children may exhibit negative behavior indicating that something is out of sync.

Reckoning

After checking with our local child support office in Tarrant County, Texas, we were informed that after this situation occurs two times, the court automatically requires the money be sent by cashier's check or money order. If the payment comes on the thirtieth day or later of the payment period, the person receiving the child support can file contempt of court through the Child Support Office. If the court determines there is deliberate intent to manipulate the court order for child support, Automatic Income Withholding may be ordered. This action takes the child support money from the payer's paychecks at their place of employment. The court may order this action even if they are receiving workman's compensation or welfare. Deliberate contempt of court may also carry with it the possibility of a jail sentence.

Competition

Warfare with an ex-mate is usually subtle and on two fronts—the present family and the ex-mate's family. For example, one parent may buy the kids a lot of gifts that are very inexpensive, while the other parent may buy fewer gifts that cost more. Another conflict may erupt over who gets to see report cards first. Or the competition may be as simple as where parents and stepparents sit during an adult child's wedding ceremony.

DON: When my son, David, and his wife, Keely, gave birth to the first of their three children, the hospital nurses were confused and felt awkward about which grandparent got to hold the grandchild first. As she looked at three sets of grandparents, one of the nurses said, "This is the largest immediate family I've ever seen. Are you sure all of you are grandparents?"

We grandparents decided to remove the barriers of competition by letting the great-great-grandparents and the great-grandmother hold the baby first. Then we took our turns without conflict.

Combat Wisdom for Dealing with Exes

Fear leads to warfare. Competition that is uncontrolled becomes combat. We are controlled by fear of what our exes *might* do, as well as by the fear of what they *are* doing. When fear is present, we tend to fight to regain control out of a sense of self-preservation.

Lenora began to question whether God knew what he was doing in her life. Two years ago her husband, Brad, divorced her despite her protests. Since she hadn't attended the court proceedings, she knew nothing about her day in court except that she was now a single parent. Recently, she was shocked when she received a summons to appear in court with Brad. He wanted their two-year-old divorce annulled on the grounds that his rights might have been violated because the divorce proceedings had not been officially recorded by a court reporter.

In the two years since the divorce, Lenora had gotten on her feet financially, had bought and furnished a home, had continued involvement with her church, and had become a self-sufficient single parent. Her personal growth during this time included dealing with and overcoming the effects of an abusive marriage. She was confused now. How could she, the "innocent party," have this happen to her, especially just when she was planning her marriage to Vince?

To be combat wise, we must not fight fire with fire; we must fight fire with faith.

Lenora was devastated when the judge said, "Sure, I'll let you be married again!" Possible implications of the judge's decision raced through her mind. It meant her marriage to Vince might not happen. She might lose her house and have to share her bank account and her life with someone she no longer loved. As she entertained these thoughts, Brad mouthed to her, "I've sold everything I owned, rented a furnished apartment, cleaned out my bank account, and I am driving an old car."

Lenora found herself climbing over the table to attack Brad, but her attorney and her brother held her back. She had been reduced to despair and fear. Knowing she could no longer live with Brad, she went into hiding. Friends from church helped her move her child and her belongings out of her house. She was terrified at the thought of Brad claiming what she had earned during the two years they were divorced.

This experience tested Lenora's faith. She was angry and bitter and unable to sleep. During those sleepless nights she began reading her Bible and praying. A friend suggested she read *Hinds' Feet on High Places,* by Hannah Hurnard (Tyndale House Publishers, 1987). She began to identify with the crippled lamb described in the book. She established a deeper relationship with God and came to terms with her situation with Brad. Without her faith she would not have heard God and would have fought Brad with the same warfare he was using on her.

Soon Lenora learned that Brad had again filed for divorce from her. In fact, he had refiled the very day the original divorce was annulled. The second divorce was granted one week later.

To be combat wise, we must not fight fire with fire; we must fight fire with faith. We can do this by

praying that we will hear and understand what God is telling us;

praying for our exes—yes, our exes—we will find it increasingly more difficult to hate the one for whom we are praying;

establishing the limits of our relationship with our exes— first, in our own minds, and then possibly verbalizing those limits to our ex-mates;

working with our exes from a position of confidence rather than of fear;

refusing to be drawn into any argumentative communication;

dealing only with the issue at hand;

developing a spirit of cooperation with our new mates on these issues.

As we seek to please God rather than ourselves or other people, we can be encouraged by James: "Consider it pure joy, my brothers, whenever you face trials of many kinds, because you know that the testing of your faith develops perseverance. Perseverance must finish its work so that you may be mature and complete, not lacking anything. If any of you lacks wisdom, he should ask God, who gives generously to all without finding fault, and it will be given to him. But when he asks, he must believe and not doubt, because he who doubts is like a wave of the sea, blown and tossed by the wind" (James 1:2–6).

The more we exercise our faith, the more we will trust God and what he is doing in our relationships with our exes. This does not mean we are trusting our exes; it means we are trusting what God is doing. There will always be caution lights alerting us to slow down or pull back from involvement in certain situations with our exes. This is selective trust. We must be sensitive to the signals God gives us concerning issues and decisions involving our ex-mates. Basing our decisions on our faith in God's direction brings inner poise and peace, which become our strength.

"Well-Fare" to "Well-Fair"

The only way to avoid warfare is to seek the help of others. We must begin personal "well-fare" by listening to people God brings into our lives who do not feed the warfare. How do we know who these people are? They will be people who trust God and trust what he is doing in people's lives. They are sensitive to signals God gives concerning the issues of life. They base their decisions on faith and they do not feed the warfare. As we filter through what God is doing in us, some of what we hear is confirmation, some is caution, and some is counsel. We must listen with compassionate Christian hearts that can discern God's voice.

When we reach a level of confidence that is based on God's empowerment, we are able to exhibit the desire to treat others, particularly our exes, with kindness and respect. We begin with our thought processes by recognizing that our exes are human beings who deserve respect.

Now we are in a position to negotiate some of the issues with which we must deal.

Negotiation

Developing skills in negotiation is a good way of becoming combat wise. In order to get, we sometimes have to give. We have found the following six steps effective when negotiating with an ex-mate:

1. Gather data to substantiate your position.
2. Focus on what is right.
3. Keep the end result in mind.
4. Listen with understanding rather than planning your response.
5. Refuse to blame or defend.
6. Follow through with decisions that have been made.

The question asked at the end of a negotiation should be, "Is everyone satisfied?" not, "Who won?"

Detachment

Detachment is another combat-wise technique. Detaching ourselves from any emotional involvement with our exes is a prerequisite to fairness. It allows us to step out of our emotional clothes into a more businesslike attitude. If we have remarried, our ability to remove the emotional shield we all seem to wear is greatly influenced by our new mate's conciliatory attitude. Our new mate's attitude can allow us to have contact with or prevent us from having contact with our ex. Prevention brings on more combat. Detachment is a form of compassion, since it allows us to deal with our exes on a more nonthreatening level, and we can begin to view them much like a distant relative.

Five Effective Habits

Regardless of our feelings about the habits we had before we were divorced, our present circumstances dictate that we form effective habits now. In his book *The Seven Habits of Highly Effective People,* Stephen Covey gives training in management principles that are easily applied to relationships, specifically with exes. We found five habits (the numbers match those in Covey's book) that seem particularly appropriate in dealing with our ex-spouses.[1]

Habit 1—Be Proactive

Covey defines *responsibility* as "the ability to choose our response to situations, making them more a product of our values and decisions than our moods and conditions." When working with our exes, the freedom to choose our responses is the deciding factor in whether or not we will be in warfare.

DON: Earlier, I described how the illness and death of my former mother-in-law gave me an opportunity to approach my ex-wife in kindness rather than suspicion. I chose my response before I went to the hospital, and that choice gave me the freedom to comfort as well as to be comforted.

Habit 2—Begin with the End in Mind

Another Covey habit is to "begin with the end in mind." We must create mentally before we act. It may be valuable to write a statement about how we are going to deal with situations involving our exes so we can remind ourselves what we desire as the outcome. This statement can help us stay within our values and priorities. Placing this statement of desired outcome close to the telephone may help us stay focused as we talk with our exes and so prevent us from entering battles.

Habit 4—Think Win-Win

According to Covey, "Win-win thinking begins with a commitment to explore all options until a mutually satisfactory solution is reached, or to make no deal at all." This thinking process allows us to explore all options with our ex-mates without being forced to make decisions with which we are uncomfortable. When there is a win-win result, both people walk away with their self-respect. This is "well-fare."

Habit 5—Seek First to Understand

Covey also suggests that we "seek first to understand, then to be understood." Feeling misunderstood often is a critical factor in divorce. Understanding an ex's point of view requires empathy, which gives the ex emotional breathing space. Understanding does not necessarily mean "agreement." Once an ex feels understood, they tend to be less defensive.

Habit 6—Synergize

Covey refers to the habit of creative cooperation or teamwork as "synergy, where the whole is greater than the sum of its parts." When different viewpoints are mutually respected, the best solution can be sought, often different than the two original ideas. If we remove our ex's reasons to protect by not attacking them, whatever decision we are trying to reach becomes possible.

Being combat wise, using negotiation skills, and developing new habits make it possible to move from warfare to "well-fare." This transition rarely happens without effort on the part of both parties. Everyone in our life space benefits when we stop the war. Stopping the war is a prerequisite for developing loving concern. Releasing control links loving concern with compassion.

Control
or Compassion

I t took two and a half years of hard struggling, but we finally were able to respect each other with kindness and to talk like two human beings. Our relationship had been so poor we had screwed up our marriage. We agreed not to screw up our son's life. We decided we would try to be friendly."

Kevin described his unusual relationship with his ex-wife, Melissa. The two of them wanted to disengage their son, Kendall, from their hurts and arguments with each other. This desire was so strong in both of them that they were able to allow the anger in their relationship to subside. They realized when they fought with each other, Kendall was affected. Compassion had a chance because they both recognized the consequences of poor behavior.

Kevin and Melissa have very similar parenting styles, which eliminated any opportunity for Kendall to manipulate his parents. He learned at an early age an important lesson for every child of divorce: When the natural parents communicate freely and often, with the child's welfare in mind, the doors to manipulation by children are closed.

Giving In for Our Children

Kevin and Melissa have a unique way of approaching their finances as a divorced couple. They were married twice and divorced twice—from each other! The first divorce had child support written into the decree. Kevin would pay with a check, which Melissa returned to him. They had a deep faith in each other's integrity regarding Kendall. Therefore, Melissa knew Kevin would take responsibility for covering his portion of Kendall's expenses. When they divorced the second time, child support was not written into the decree. Both of them pay one-half of Kendall's expenses. The absence of forced payments has given them the freedom to pay more than child support would have been. There seems to be no resentment in either Kevin or Melissa with this agreement. They have a special bond built on mutual respect that has developed into loving concern.

Melissa tells how this bond developed:

I remember the conversation Kevin and I had at our second separation when we made the decision to remember the divorce was not Kendall's fault. Our main goal was to think of him first. We decided that Kendall could not suffer because of our situation. We both took that commitment seriously, and in moments of anger at each other, we have kept Kendall's welfare in mind.

The hardest issue to resolve in a divorce concerns money. However the money is divided, it seems as if our exes get more than we do. When Kevin and I dissolved our business, I felt the settlement was unfair. I was in counseling, and my counselor asked me:

"Is that something you can live with?"

"Yes, but I don't think it's fair!" I replied.

My counselor repeated: "I know, but is that something you can live with?" At that point, I chose to think of the situation as an investment in my son's life through an amicable relationship with Kevin. I accepted the settlement.

When I don't want to bend on an issue, but it's no big deal, I remember I'm investing in Kendall's future. I'm not giving in to Kevin but giving in *for* Kendall.

Divorce often results in parents playing tug-of-war, with their children in the middle. When both parents focus on the welfare of the children, they can stop tugging on the rope and simply move toward the children. The anger may stay for a while, but they keep renewing their commitment to their sons and daughters.

When Kevin married Madelaine, Melissa liked her immediately. She wrote Madelaine a letter of appreciation for being a kind and fair stepmother to Kendall. Melissa was investing even more in Kendall's future by this act of compassion. She realized that any turmoil in Kevin and Madelaine's household was not good for Kendall, and since Melissa also has stepchildren, she wanted to be as positive as possible with her new family.

Madelaine fosters compassion by supporting the relationship between Kevin and Melissa. Madelaine's investment is first in her marriage to Kevin and then in her relationship with Kendall. It is so easy for a new wife or husband to try exercising control by not allowing the relationship between their spouse and his or her ex to exist. However, that resistant attitude always leads to discord in the lives of all concerned.

Kevin and Melissa have another unique factor in their relationship—trust. Trust must be developed in the same way as compassion. Many exes may be unable to develop as much trust as Kevin and Melissa have done. For a divorced person, trust is harder to build than compassion, and it is not as necessary for our own emotional health as is compassion. Compassion is a decision we make about our feelings. We cannot experience compassion until we have overcome hate. Compassion creates an atmosphere of giving rather than taking. Trust, on the other hand, involves another person's actions and attitudes, making it conditional. Therefore, we can only exercise trust to the degree our exes are trustworthy.

Throughout Scripture we are instructed to trust in God and to love and have compassion for each other. "It is better to trust in the LORD than to put confidence in man" (Psalm 118:8 KJV). "Trust in the LORD with all your heart and lean not on your own understanding" (Proverbs 3:5). The more we trust God, the more compassion we are able to extend toward our exes. "Therefore, as God's chosen people, holy and dearly loved, clothe yourselves with compassion, kindness, humility, gentleness and patience" (Colossians 3:12).

Compassion Is Not Pity

Kevin and Melissa made a committed decision to control their own emotions and actions rather than trying to control each other. When we give up our desire to control other people, we can begin to develop compassion for them. Compassion is not pity or some tearfully sentimental feeling for our exes. Compassion is feeling sympathy for their hurt, whether or not they caused it themselves. When dealing with an ex, our compassion level may be great, but often the amount of help we offer is limited by our particular situation. For an ex, our desire to help could be . . . not to make it any worse.

Things We Can't Control

We don't all need to get along as well as Kevin and Melissa, but we can function effectively at a lesser level of trust. All divorced people are aware that their control is limited when it comes to their exes. Ex-mates are free to do whatever they want with their possessions, their lives, and their children when they are with them. We cannot control how our exes and their family members treat us. We can choose to stew all the time over what we cannot control, or we can get over it and get on with life.

> *We must get beyond feelings of loss or of need to control.*

DON: My ex-wife entered our "ex-house" several times after we were divorced and removed items that I highly valued, and there seemed to be nothing that I could do about it. Her actions were a dramatic, physical symbol that left me feeling as if she still controlled some part of my life. It took me many years to let go of the bitterness. I made a conscious choice to exhibit compassion even though my trust in her was limited.

The details involved in Don's scenario will be different from those in your life, but the feelings of loss of control are probably the same. When we feel controlled by outside people or forces, we often experience anger and depression.

Getting beyond the Need to Control

We must get beyond feelings of loss or of need to control. We begin this process by accepting the fact that the things we have lost from our past are gone for good. Once we give up the expectations of getting them back, we can deal with our feelings about exes taking them. The next step is to determine where we are in the control issue—controlling or being controlled.

DON: I found myself playing the "poor me" song as if I were being controlled, when in reality that was my way of trying to control the whole situation. The greatest controller was the effect anger and bitterness had in my life. To get out from under the thumb of anger and bitterness, it was necessary for me to give up the pity party and get on with life. Getting beyond having to control brings the freedom to begin compassion.

Compassion Is a Decision

Compassion is a decision to work toward a feeling of concern and understanding. There are limits to how much we can help our exes. We may have a high level of understanding and concern and may wish to help a lot, but our ability to help is limited by the feelings our exes have toward us.

One powerful decision we can make is to pray for our exes. It is very difficult to hate someone for whom we are praying. We don't have to feel affectionate toward our exes, but we must remember that "God has not given us a spirit of timidity, but of power and love and discipline" (2 Timothy 1:7 NASB). This enables us to embrace the freedom to care for our exes' welfare. This should not be confused with any degree of intimacy. Our prayers draw us closer to God and enable us to see clearly our limits in relationship to our exes.

Compassion in Action

We do not give compassion in order to get compassion because we may never receive compassion from our exes. We are not trying to please our exes; we are seeking to please our Lord. Here are several things we can do to express compassion for our exes:

Listen more than we talk.

Acknowledge that our exes have opinions and ask them to share them. "What do you think?" "How do you feel?" This doesn't mean we have to agree with or value their opinions. For example: "I'm glad you have shared that with me." "Thank you for helping me understand."

Acknowledge our exes' pain. For example: "I'm sorry you're hurting that way." "I understand that can make you sad."

Do not use verbal or emotional warfare. Don't use what we know about our exes to push their buttons and bring up past hurts.

We need to practice these things regardless of the reaction of our exes. Whether they accuse us of manipulation, question our motives, curse us, or hang up on us, we can remain steadfast in the strength of the Lord. "When you are reviled and persecuted and lied about because you are my followers—wonderful! Be happy about it! Be very glad! for a tremendous reward awaits you up in heaven. And remember, the ancient prophets were persecuted too" (Matthew 5:11–12 TLB).

We may find that through our willingness to be compassionate, our exes may begin to show some feelings of compassion also. Often they will go through the same process of growth we have been through and will want to get on with their lives.

The World of Ex-Hood

Whether we are dealing with the ex-mate of our new spouse or the new spouse of our ex-mate, we have entered the world of "ex-hood." Both of these persons are in the noncontrol area of our lives, although they can exert a strong influence on our families. Whenever our mates resent or are jealous of our contact with our exes, it contributes to a lack of household harmony and inhibits the mental and emotional well-being of any children involved.

LADEAN: My ex-husband, George, and I have been able to maintain harmony by sharing on-campus lunches with our son, Trey, while he has been a busy college student. These special times, which have been very good for us, would not have been possible if Don and Paulette, George's wife, were not agreeable to these lunches. Their concern for Trey's welfare was combined with confidence that neither George nor I would compromise our marriages by being together.

We have had to deal with our ex-mates in very different ways. I feel that my presence causes feelings of competition when we are at family gatherings involving Don and his ex-wife. Don's children were in their twenties when they divorced, and the need for Don and Beverly to work together on finances, education issues, and other parenting situations was not there, thus making cooperation a slower process. Our grandchildren have been the catalyst for bringing about their willingness to get along. There is great cooperation and freedom on one side of our ex-hood and some limitations on the other side. Don and I both feel the same compassion for our exes, but only in recent months have we become more comfortable expressing our compassion for Don's ex-wife.

Our lives, and those of people who shared their experiences with us, testify that children represent the greatest need for exes to communicate and cooperate.

Petty or Partners

LADEAN: I felt as if I were in a Chevy Chase movie. Don and I along with my ex-husband and his wife were all doing the drum major strut on the twenty-yard line of the football field at Texas Christian University on Parents' Day. We followed our drum major son Trey down to the fifty-yard line as other band parents marched with their children, sharing one of the fun traditions at TCU—marching with band members as they practice their halftime routine. The four of us waddled like ducks in a row behind Trey as he led the band.

"Trey," I gasped, "I've always wanted to do my high school drill team high kick on this football field, and now I'm here! This is neat!"

"Mom, this is not the drill team. Please try to act like a drum major!"

The five of us must have been a sight, since the other parents were taking pictures and laughing at Trey's four unlikely tagalongs. The band director noted over his bullhorn that Trey had surely won the prize for having the most parents present for the festivities. Even more amazing is the fact that after Trey and the band broke up to meet other obligations, the four parents drove to a restaurant for the world's greatest pancakes and had breakfast together. What a way to have completed Trey's Saturday saga of "All My Parents"!

I would be the first to admit that day was almost a fairy-tale situation. The long and winding road from where this saga began to where we are today has been an adventurous one. Trey's dad and I are not the same people who left divorce court years ago. I can still remember the feelings of fear, embarrassment, guilt, anger, and frustration that I experienced during the divorce proceedings. Trying to gain some order in my life at that time was definitely a gut-wrenching experience. It was the worst time of my life, but I never want to forget how much I discovered about myself and how much I have grown since those days.

Obviously, God's will for his people to experience growth doesn't mean he wants divorce. We believe God earnestly desires us to grow within marriage into all he wishes us to be. Those of us who are divorced understand why God hates it, but we are also very aware of how much God loves the people involved. He loves us long before and through our repentance, and his forgiveness makes us feel valuable to him and to ourselves.

When no children are involved in a divorce, ex-hood requires little or no contact with each other. However, when children are involved, parenting becomes a critical issue for exes, and the complications are intensified because of the fragility of the children. This makes it all the more urgent for us to be partners in parenting rather than having a "petty party."

Revenge

LADEAN: The first indication that I was turning a corner was when I realized I no longer had any feelings of desire for revenge toward my ex-husband.

The greatest evidence of pettiness between exes is revenge, and there are many ways to get it. For example, if we can get our kids to like us more than they like our exes, we feel that we have "won." This competition is a contributing factor in the "Disneyland parent" syndrome. Parents may allow the kids to get by with things they know are wrong in order to be popular with them. Exes may use any situation to get at each other. At one of our conferences, we heard the following story:

> Perry bought a car for his son Bobby, who lived with his mother, Sue.
>   Sue said, "Bobby, if you violate curfew, I'll take the keys."
>   Perry told Bobby, "Your mom can't tell you what to do with your car. I bought it for you. Park it in the street. That's a public place, and she can't touch it."

Had these parents been partners rather than being involved in petty revenge, they would have realized this was an opportunity to constructively shape Bobby's attitude toward authority. Instead, there were no winners in this situation. Being partners means equal say in the business of raising the children. As long as the parents keep the welfare of the children as their priority, there can be a working agreement.

Other issues parents commonly use to carry out revenge on each other are conflicts over children's hair length and style, brands and styles of clothing, amount of allowance, schoolwork, or dating. As long as these issues are used as weapons by the parents, the children will become pawns, and everyone loses. We often focus on the children as victims in these situations, but the adults lose as well. The anger and bitterness we harbor toward our ex-mates may even be taken out on our current families. Unfortunately, in families where ex bashing has occurred, we often see children leaving home sooner—they often marry earlier, run away, or go off to live on their own. When these children leave home, often they do not come back, because of the pain involved in touching their past. When memories are filled with controversy, it is natural to want to flee that controversy.

Some children play the divide-and-conquer game. If parents allow it, the children, often unwittingly, will keep parents at each other in order to get their way. As long as parents communicate and agree on handling issues regarding their children, the kids cannot pit one parent against the other. Parents must understand that even the best of children may be master manipulators, and when they are seeking to find their niche in the new family structure, they will make the most of parents who do not talk to each other.

Revenge is also one of the areas where grandparents tend to be victimized by being denied contact with grandchildren. Only in recent years have grandparents been able to get legal visitation rights. Revenge brings hurt to the special people in our lives. It must be put behind us. With God's help it can be. Paul instructed the Roman believers, "Do not repay anyone evil for evil. Be careful to do what is right in the eyes of everybody. If it is possible, as far as it depends on you, live at peace with everyone" (Romans 12:17–18).

Pain of the Past

We have some friends in Tennessee who are prime examples of parents who have allowed the pain of the past to destroy the present. Bill and Marilyn divorced twenty-two years ago in a bitter battle over material wealth and child custody. The lives of the families on both sides have been characterized by pettiness, hatred, and using the children as pawns as the ex-mates battled each other. There has been constant character assassination as each parent has tried to prove his or her point with the children. They have undermined each other constantly in issues dealing with the children. Any situation was fair game to the parents. They used such issues as parental authority, education, cars, curfews, and money allotment to vent their anger and bitterness toward each other. In addition, the extended family became part of the problem rather than part of the solution. When aunts, uncles, cousins, and grandparents joined in the battle of ex bashing, the children lost even more.

The last time we saw Bill, neither of us recognized him. He looked twenty-five years older than he really is. He who had been a very athletic man is now a white-haired, stooped old man. He moves around slowly and is merely a shell of the physical specimen he once was. As long as we carry our past hurt and pain with us, our revenge takes its destructive force out on *us*—not only on our exes for whom it was intended. Also, we lose credibility with those around us, especially our children, when we continue to wallow in old hurts and situations. These old wounds have no bearing on what is happening today; the past can't be changed. Continually rehashing it only reveals to others how small we are and how shallow our lives are. Our families and our friends want us to pull ourselves together and grow in new directions. In 2 Corinthians 5:17, we are encouraged to remember that we are "a brand new person inside." We are "not the same any more. A new life has begun!" (TLB).

The Dilemma Children

In Ephesians, Paul instructs children to "obey your parents in the Lord, for this is right. 'Honor your father and mother'—which is the first commandment with a promise—'that it may go well with you and that you may enjoy long life on the earth'" (6:1–2). In Perry and Sue's story, which parent should Bobby obey? The "dilemma children" are caught in a situation that attacks their understanding and acceptance of authority. Bobby cannot win.

> *Research has shown that the children of ex-mates who are hospitable to each other are healthier— mentally, emotionally, and physically.*

Whomever he obeys, he violates the other parent's authority. Bobby experienced a double dose of frustration because his parents' pettiness caused him to lose respect for both of them.

There is a generation issue involved here. These children will mature and bear children. Their confused origins and lack of respect for authority may cause them to be unable to raise children who have a healthy understanding of authority. People raised with this void in their lives may have difficulty submitting to the authority of God. Our best hope for these children is that we may be able to model parenting skills that exhibit God's parenting. Children must have positive role models in order to learn respect for authority.

Furthermore, as young children grow older, they will be forced to choose which battling parent attends which function, even if the choice is disagreeable to the parents. Research has shown that the children of ex-mates who are hospitable to each other are healthier—mentally, emotionally, and physically.

Allowing God to rule in our lives has provided a strong foundation for Trey. He is not placed in a dilemma concerning his parents. Knowing that his mom and dad are partners in decisions regarding him has given him a sense of security and stability.

The Cautious Involvement Approach

When we give our best to the relationship with our exes, we can live with ourselves, regardless of the results. We can be Christlike and work very closely as partners but allow ourselves the freedom to disengage when we feel the need to protect ourselves. If an ex begins to manipulate a situation in a destructive way, it may be prudent to withdraw from involvement. We are preventing ourselves and our children from becoming entangled in an emotionally or spiritually damaging circumstance. This is one of the real freedoms the Lord gives us as we grow in him. To some this withdrawing may seem like a cold approach, but all of us should trust in the power of the Holy Spirit to guide us so we do not make foolish and harmful decisions for our children or for ourselves.

I'm the Only One Who Wants to Work

What do we do when our exes do not want to be partners regarding the children? Perhaps we should pray the following prayer:

Lord, give me the patience to accept the things I cannot change; the courage to change the things I can; and the wisdom to know the difference.

Saint Francis of Assisi

When unilateral decisions must be made, it is a good idea to get someone else's viewpoint, perhaps a trusted friend, pastor, counselor, or teacher.

We have friends in central Texas who experienced some tough times when one ex-mate refused to be a partner concerning the children. Betty ended up with the house after the divorce. The three college-age children remained in the house when Betty remarried and moved into her new husband's home. When Betty decided to sell her ex-house, her ex-husband, Allen, informed the children that all proceeds from the sale of the house were to be divided among the children. When they asked their mother for their share of the money, she was shocked and told them, "If I don't spend the money, it will become your inheritance."

On hearing these words, the children's sense of entitlement turned to bitterness and distrust, and they did not speak to her for several months. It took years for Betty to rebuild the trust of her children. There were no issues this couple entered into concerning the children that were not sabotaged. No matter how hard Betty worked at building a partnership regarding the children, Allen seemed determined to destroy any harmony in the process.

That is when Betty came to us, and we encouraged her to begin a unilateral program that would benefit the children. A unilateral program means that we do what God intends for us to do to maintain a positive attitude about our exes. We have no control over our exes or how they respond to what we do, but we refuse to bad-mouth or undermine them in any way. This also means sometimes we have to work around them by emphasizing to the children the values, actions, and requirements we have in our homes that may be different from the ex's household. For example, we might say: "In our home, we treat people with kindness." We can leave off the obvious tag, "even if your dad/mom does not." As Betty put these principles into practice, she was able to keep herself focused on solutions even if her ex refused to cooperate.

A Plan for Partnership

Pardon

Pardoning the other person means we must exercise forgiveness. Forgiveness does not mean we desire intimate relationships with our exes. It *does* mean we cease using an ex's past actions to justify our actions, past or present. Jesus speaks plainly regarding this situation: "For if you forgive men when they sin against you, your heavenly Father will also forgive you. But if you do not forgive men their sins, your Father will not forgive your sins" (Matthew 6:14–15). It is very difficult to pardon anyone else if we cannot forgive ourselves. After a divorce, it is often difficult to forgive ourselves for whatever we think we did or did not do. We can carry blame for the breakup of the family and for traumatizing the children. Christians often carry an additional burden of feeling they are un-Christian for even being divorced. Whether or not it is entirely true, you feel responsible for not being able to work through your marriage problems. All these feelings can produce a large-economy-size guilt trip.

Society places blame for our failures on our past. The only freedom we can depend on for our feelings is from Christ. Whatever we feel we have done to hurt others and ourselves can be forgiven. In 1 John we are told that "If we confess our sins, he is faithful and just and will forgive us our sins and purify us from all unrighteousness" (1:9). This indicates we can have real freedom from the guilt we have been carrying. This is good news!

Patch

To begin patching a relationship with our ex-mates we must put our hurts behind us.

LADEAN: When George and I met for the first time to discuss Trey's junior high years, the meeting at a local restaurant concluded with George saying, "I can't believe you conducted this meeting like you have. You talked only about Trey. I can't believe you didn't bring up the past."

Because I was becoming a new me, I realized there had to be some repair of the relationship so we could effectively deal with Trey. I worked from a written agenda of topics so I would not forget why we were there. We met in a neutral place, a local restaurant, so we would not act ugly toward each other. By structuring the meeting with Trey's welfare in mind, I could approach George in a new way also.

Another area that must be patched concerns whether our ex is a Christian. If so, then he or she is our brother or sister in Christ. Our exes have the same value to God that we have, and we must respect them as believers. Praying positively for our exes can change our attitudes toward them. As we begin to realize they have value, we can accept their viewpoints as valid. If our exes are not Christians, we can still pray for them to have a soft heart and for spiritual protection for our children.

Participate

Good intentions are no substitute for action. It does not matter how many times either one of the exes thinks about doing what is best for the children; it will not happen until one person begins the process. We may have to begin the process many times, but keep in mind, we are dealing with the welfare of our children. We must not let ourselves be distracted from our objective: healthy children. Failure usually follows the path of least persistence. Being persistent allows God to change the lives of all involved—including ourselves. We may modify our plans, but we should never give up on the plan God has given us or on what we believe is best for our children. When participation is a partnership, all family members get to enjoy the child's activities.

Shared participation also includes confronting the child. It is best for both natural parents to agree on what actions should be taken regarding long-range consequences, character development, value determination, and relationship skills. For example, parents should consider how they want to deal with problems related to curfews, authority, finances, and school. By turning to God for direction, forgetting our pettiness, and working together to benefit our children, we can see positive changes.

Strength of Character

We need a structured plan to work with our exes in parenting. Parenting is always challenging and for divorced parents even more so. The challenges are magnified when natural parents are unable to put aside their differences long enough to work for the best interest of their children. Here are seven suggestions for fostering partnership parenting with your ex.

1. Communicate frequently with each other about the child. Let the child know you are talking with the other natural parent.
2. Discuss options with each other before making decisions.
3. Don't sabotage the other parent or the joint decisions you've made.
4. Don't keep secrets; don't ask the child not to tell Mom/Dad about something.
5. Don't make the child have to choose which parent to include in their activities; be amiable enough that both natural parents could attend.
6. Support the special areas of interest your ex may have with your child, rather than compete with them. For example, music was an interest LaDean and Trey enjoyed. George encouraged but never tried to compete in that discipline. George and Trey participated in In-

dian Guides, a YMCA program for fathers and sons, and LaDean supported that relationship without trying to compete with a similar program.

7. Let the love for your child be more important than your individual desires. Be willing to work with each other.

Divorced parenting requires that we exhibit characteristics we don't want to exhibit toward our exes, like patience, kindness, understanding, and acceptance. These actions require strength of character—our strength of character. The consequences are too costly when we refuse to change our attitudes. We are encouraged as we see more and more adults who are willing to put their concerns for their child above their individual irritations.

If at First—or Second or Third—You Don't Succeed

What if we try to get along and our exes don't contribute at all? Do we give up? Do we get angry? Do we call them dirty rotten scoundrels? Or do we continue trying because of our faith in what the Lord is doing in our lives? As we listen and learn, we can be aware of our feelings and yet continue working with our exes in a godly manner—regardless of their responses. Faith and conviction become stronger when attacked. No, we don't give up. Yes, we may get angry, but we don't stay angry. Yes, we may think of them as dirty rotten scoundrels, but it's probably best not to call them that. Yes, we keep remembering that our faith must be in God and his plan for us rather than focusing on what our exes may or may not be doing.

What do we do when we try all we can and nothing seems to be improving? There are those situations when we feel we are hitting a brick wall. What do we do? Sometimes we must go around or over obstacles. Other times we must go on with life and hope our exes catch up. This doesn't mean we break off all communication, but we cannot stay in a vacuum forever. When we disconnect, but they won't cooperate, it can leave a vacant place in our lives. What God wants from us is the desire and effort to have a congenial relationship with our exes. "We can justify our every deed but God looks at our motives" (Proverbs 21:2 TLB).

When we have done all we can do, and there is no response from our exes, they are responsible to God for their actions. We should be flexible, cooperative, and communicative, but we cannot be dragged down in life if they refuse to cooperate. When we let ourselves get angry and upset with them, we give them a part of us, and sometimes we need to go on living as if they are not there. This may not be the most desirable result, but it is an alternative to an unresponsive ex-mate.

God is not always going to change our circumstances when we cry out to him. However, he always has the goal of changing us to view our ex-mates from his perspective. The more we allow the Holy Spirit to work in us, the clearer our perspective becomes concerning situations with our exes. As we daily practice faith in action, we become wiser in sorting through the issues of our past and present lives, and it becomes easier for us to determine what to hold on to and what to let go of.

A Closing Blessing

All growth brings about change. Sometimes growth is painful, especially to our emotions and egos. If you are not content with where your life is, then you must choose to change. We have barraged you with information. You may feel God is asking a lot of you to think and act differently toward your ex-mate. Begin where God has revealed your greatest need, and change that attitude or action in your life before going to the next revelation. It sometimes takes years to get where we need to be, but the journey is both the work and the joy. Remember, you are doing this for your own mental, emotional, and spiritual health as well as for your children's welfare. God's will is for us to have the mind of Christ. Let us arm ourselves with new resolve to be lights, to build bridges, to be tolerant, to be compassionate, and to approach our ex-mates from now on in ways that please God. We leave you with this blessing:

May God burn into your heart the biblical principles that will bring change and victory to your life.

May you accept the challenge to do something about what you have read—to treat your ex as Christ would.

May your children become healthy adults who can love both their parents without feeling disloyal, and may they see a new strength in their parents that they can desire and anchor onto themselves.

Finally, may you find through the work of the Holy Spirit the ability to be tough enough to be kind, strong enough to be gentle, and powerful enough to be compassionate.

Recommended Resources

Reluctantly Single by Harold Ivan Smith (Nashville: Abingdon Press, 1994).

When Your Children Divorce by Elaine R. Seppa (Downers Grove, Ill.: InterVarsity Press, 1995).

When Your Ex Won't Pay by Nancy S. Palmer and Ana Tangel-Rodriguez (Colorado Springs: Pinon, 1995).

Notes

Chapter 2: *A Light or a Judge*

1. Stephen Covey, *Principle-Centered Leadership* (New York: Simon & Schuster, 1991), 25.

Chapter 4: *Barriers or Bridges*

1. *Macmillan's Dictionary* (New York: Macmillan, 1977), 849.

Chapter 6: *Conflict or Creativity*

1. Gary Smalley and John Trent, *Leaving the Light On* (Portland, Ore.: Multnomah, 1994), 63.
2. Ibid., 28.

Chapter 7: *Bitter or Better*

1. Don and LaDean Houck, *Remarried with Children* (San Bernardino: Here's Life Publishers, Inc., 1991), 76, 190.

Chapter 8: *Warfare or "Well-fare"*

1. Stephen Covey, *The Seven Habits of Highly Effective People* (New York: Simon & Schuster, 1990), 65, 71, 97, 207, 235, 262, 263.

Blended Blessings

I n 1984, we began our ministry, called Blended Blessings, to blended families and to divorced singles who were planning to remarry. After struggling three years in our own blended family, we desired to help others walk a smoother road. We have a threefold purpose for Blended Blessings: to keep the current marriage intact, to break the cycle of divorce, and to restore the family unit to harmony.

Because nearly everyone's life is touched in some way by divorce and remarriage, many churches have found the principles we teach are pertinent to their entire congregations. Our conferences are tailored to meet the specific needs of the audience to which we speak. Our first book, *Remarried with Children* (Here's Life Publishers, Inc., 1991), evolved from the workshops we have conducted throughout the United States. We have found that dealing with ex-hood is an opportunity to exercise a major point of grace after a divorce.

To contact us, write: Blended Blessings, 4101 Green Oaks Boulevard West, Suite 207, Arlington, TX 76016.